What Readers are Saying...

"Imagine what will happen to our economy when more women become money savvy and bring *HarMoney* into their relationships, their businesses, and even the political arena. Renée's gutsy storytelling shows us we're not alone. Gaining control really is simple for us to do when we decide to empower our own lives…our own selves. Reneé tells us how she did it. We'd be wise to listen. *HarMoney* is a real treasure!"

— **The Honorable Mary Bono**
Member of Congress (1998-2013),
Senior Vice-President, FaegreBD Consulting

"Renée shares her own personal financial parable of how poor money habits developed during childhood can spill into adulthood to create what feels like an inescapable financial hole. Sound familiar? Despair not. Renée shows us how those faced with great adversity — even serious brain injury — can gain control over their finances and find harmony. It's a combination she calls 'HarMoney™.' How can you get there? Align your money behavior with your values and goals. Adopt transparent systems to keep you and your family on track and to build mutual trust. Be grateful for what you have. 'Fail forward' by forgiving yourself and learning from your mistakes. Ask for help. Where can you find help that's practical and non-judgmental? Start with Renée's book."

— Bill Dwight
CEO and Founder of FamZoo.com
(the award winning online system that helps parents teach kids good money habits)

"A lack of sound financial education has led to our economic struggle. It is our responsibility to become money savvy so that we may empower others to be free from financial oppression. Renée has gone to the depths of vulnerability to share her journey with you. The lessons and wisdom she shares in this piece will elevate you to a new level of understanding your relationship with money, providing you a clear path to freedom in all areas of your life. This is one book you will recommend to anyone seeking financial peace of mind."

— Savannah-Brooklyn Ross
Speaker, Investor, Founder of Rich Mom Enterprises

"Renée has courageously shared her story of overcoming financial obstacles and the lessons she learned along the journey. By revealing her own learning experiences, Renée sheds light on the incredible role that mindset has in creating financial success."

— **Sharon Lechter**
   Founder and CEO, Pay Your Family First
   Co-Author of *Rich Dad Poor Dad, Three Feet from Gold, Outwitting the Devil*
   Author of *Save Wisely, Spend Happily*

"Finally! Someone with the guts to SHOW you how it's done, not just harp on old clichés. Renée's been there and come back, and she's living proof that you can come back too! Her simple, 'define your own rules' approach to developing a HarMoneyous™ relationship with your money puts YOU in charge, making it easy for you (and your partner) to start right now, creating the joyful, fulfilling future you desire. Take the first step and devour *HarMoney*. Then get to work on the rest of your wonderful life."

— **Nancy Langdon Jones, CFP®**
   Author of *So You Want to Be a Financial Planner*
   Mentor, American Business Women's Association 2003 Top Ten

"Making things better and not giving up is what Make-A-Wish® is all about, and so is Renée's message. In her heart-wrenching story, she reveals how her triumph over catastrophic injury and broken financial stories, led her to motivate others to keep going when all seems to be lost and give them a simple process to follow. *HarMoney* is a real game-changer for your mind and your money!"

—Frank Shankwitz
Founder, Make-A-Wish® Foundation

"In our society today, no one wants to talk about money. And yet, with disappearing pensions and an uncertain future for Social Security, this is the exact time that we all need to dive deeply into the 'money game.' In her book, *HarMoney*, Renée gives us a front row seat into her own life — her personal struggles and ultimate triumphs in the area of money. Plus, Renée shares a personal tragedy that almost cost her everything, and how she was able to recover from that while retraining her brain to master the simplest tasks and then taking a quantum leap to write this book, launch a new business, and expand her own conversation about money and abundance. This book is a must read for anyone who is tired of their old money stories and is ready to build the future they've been dreaming about using Renée's simple step-by-step process."

—Ursula Mentjes
Two-time #1 Bestselling Author of *Selling with Intention & Selling with Synchronicity*

"Renée really is a 'Miracle in Action!' What a perfect time to hear a story of turning crisis and pain into power, peace, and joy. In this book, Renée shares her simple HarMoney™ method so you can turn your situation around and triumph as well!"

— **Angela Alexander**
Author of *Miracles in Action* and
Inspirational Speaker

"Who knew, when I started coaching Renée through the process of writing this book four years ago, that it would be her expertise that would save my financial future and, more importantly, my marriage. Thanks to Renée, my husband and I have hope that we can create an abundant future for our family and tools and strategies to make it happen. Thank you, Renée!"

— **Amanda Johnson**
Founder of True to Intention, Speaker,
Upside-Down MessagePreneur™ Coach, and
#1 Bestselling Author of *Upside-Down Mommy*

"Renée's story of recovery and renewal in the face of a traumatic brain injury is inspirational. She has met the challenges of rehabilitation with openness and courage. With wisdom and compassion, she has applied the lessons learned to the financial challenges we all face."

— **Karen Salter-Moss, Ph.D.**
Clinical Neuropsychologist

"Renée has taken a subject that can often bring up fear and stress, and has made it exciting and motivating. She gives the reader tools for understanding money, and the inspiration to be driven forward to increased success with it. This is a truly magnificent book on soaring to new heights with your finances, profits, and money manifesting."

—Kim Somers Egelsee
Life Coach, Inspirational Speaker, #1 Bestselling Author of *Getting Your Life to a Ten*

"Renée has truly taken the money conversation to a whole new level of real, simple, and doable that I didn't even know existed! By revealing her own journey of money misconceptions and the priceless wisdom that she discovered along the way, she has opened my eyes to a deeper understanding that it's about so much more than money — it's my mindset. Her perseverance and unwillingness to settle for less is a testament that anyone can get their financial house in order because of the tools that Renée has developed. This is an absolute must-read for anyone who longs for *HarMoney* in their lives!"

—Marlia Cochran
Transformational Speaker, Author of *Where's My White Picket Fence: When A Good Girl Doubts God*, Radio Co-Host, and Founder of Good Girl Enterprises

"WOW! Like Renée, I never was taught the basic skills of saving money. I knew how to earn it, but save it? Forget it! Reading *HarMoney* gave me an insight of how important it is to discover your personal values to achieve financial, personal, professional, and relational success. Renée is a driven woman who simply wants to educate others on how to be Money Savvy to find HarMoney. Being an advocate for victims of domestic violence, I see a lot of financial insecurities and struggles. After all, they leave with nothing. I plan on sharing this book with those women and children. *HarMoney* is an easy read and offers phenomenal basic life skills that will empower others to gain financial control. *HarMoney* will, with no doubt, empower everyone. Thank you, Renée, for giving me the confidence to make some changes in my life and to help others do the same. Huge Hugs!"

—**Tanya L. Brown**
   Sister of the late Nicole Brown Simpson
   Inspirational Speaker on Promoting Mental Wellness
   and Domestic Violence Prevention, Life Skills
   Coach and Author of *Finding Peace Amid The
   Chaos: My Escape From Depression and Suicide*
   Creator of the "The Sneaky Seven Characters of
   Abuse and Tanya's Tools For Change"

"What a sobering and inspiring read! Renée has captured the pain and struggles that so many people face in search of financial wellness but have been afraid to admit. Through Renee's transparency and passion to help others, you will discover that you are not alone in your struggle, but that there is a solution. Renee's *HarMoney* gives you the transforming process to break the cycles that have blocked your financial freedom. This book spoke to me on so many levels, and if you are ready to change your Money Game, *HarMoney* will speak to you as well and encourage you to take action now."

— **Gwen Thibeaux, M.A.**
  Life Empowerment Coach, Speaker,
  and Author of *Embracing the Greatness Within:
  A Journey of Purpose and Passion*

"Finally, here is an enjoyable, easy-to-read book about money and its relationships to personal values. This little gem puts action and control in the readers' hands. You will laugh at yourself, maybe shed a tear, but you will move forward to taking control of your money as you follow along on this journey. Everyone seeking financial freedom, especiallly new couples, and old ones too, will discover it's not all about a painful budget. It can be 'Your money, your way!'"

— **Cheryle L. Steddom, CPA, CVA**
  Steddom Accountancy,
  A Professional Corporation

"I highly praise Renée Cabourne for her courage in writing this must-read book. We all have our own journey when it comes to money. She has taken her journey and used it to share her wisdom with others. I commend her for her focus on educating her clients in order to motivate them to make positive change with their money. This is more than a book about money; it is also a book about communication and relationships. I would highly recommend it to any of my clients."

—Suzanne M. Graves
Law Offices of Suzanne M. Graves, Inc.
Co-Author of Strictly Business; Love, Money, and Control; The Complete Guide to Estate and Financial Planning in Turbulent Times; and Being in Business Is A Funny Thing—Getting Out Is Not!

"I got goose bumps while reading *HarMoney: Your Money…Your Rules, Your Way!* We all wind up facing seemingly impossible barriers and obstacles, and feel like quitting a lot of the time. Winners never do. They find a way to persevere. Renée reveals, through her inspiring story, how you can overcome defeat and grow from 'toddler' to 'adulthood' with her simple HarMoney™ process. If you want to find a winning mindset around money, this book was written for you!"

—Brian Smith
UGG Australia Founder

"From the first page, I felt that *HarMoney* was talking directly to me. Financial literacy tends to be a dry subject. Finally, someone gets how to write a financial literacy book that is attention-grabbing, interesting, and educational. The anecdotal stories were heartfelt and entertaining. I could relate them to my own life. It made me laugh, it made me cry, it made me think."

—Sandra Rutherford
> Executive Director of Council Services, Camp Fire Inland Southern California

"I started reading *HarMoney* with the mindset of it being another spin on managing money. What I found was an inspiring, funny, get your hands in the dirt guide to changing your relationship with money! Renée Cabourne reveals not only "Her Story" which so many can relate to, but a practical, easy, step-by-step guide to "HarMoney."

Part comedian, part intellectual. part marriage counselor, and full-on successful money coach, Renée's book will have you laughing, crying, thinking, and doing from the first page to the last!"

—Kelli Holmes
> TEAM Referral Network Founder and CEO

"As an Olympic athlete, I was constantly striving for the highest level of success while trying to figure out how to have it all. As a woman, a mom, and often an employee or businesswoman, we want to be successful, but often don't know how to get there. In *HarMoney*, Renée lays out a plan to help find success as you take charge of your finances. This book teaches how to become more financially successful while giving important tips on how to reach those goals. This book will be refreshing to you or anyone who wants to become better stewards of their hard-earned money."

—Leah Amico
3-Time Olympic Gold Medalist with USA Softball, Speaker, Softball Commentator for ESPN

HarMoney

A Step-by-Step Guide
To Your Money…

Your Rules, Your Way!

by

Renée E. Cabourne, CFP®
Money Savvy Woman, Inc.

HarMoney™
A Step-by-Step Guide To Your Money…
Your Rules, Your Way!

Published by
Money Savvy Woman, Inc.
La Verne, California

www.MoneySavvyWoman.com

Cover Illustration by Michelle Ball
Cover Design by Dan Mulhern Design
Interior Design by Dawn Teagarden
Photography by Robbie Snider of RL Photography

ISBN: 978-0-9910465-0-8 (paperback)

Printed in the United States of America

www.MoneySavvyWoman.com

Dedicated...
To my parents,
Buddy and Mary Riedel

Dad, it's true we couldn't agree that the sky was blue, but when it was written, "All things work together for the glory of God," (Romans 8:28), He had to be talking about you and me. I love you, Dad, more with every passing day. My greatest and hardest lessons were learned at your hand. Some were the most brutal, but some were the most loving. Without my faith in Christ Jesus, the greatest gift you ever shared, I would certainly be nothing. Some, when they read this, may think I've wronged you by openly telling our story, but I don't think so. I believe you've sent me clear messages from above guiding me along the way, allowing me the freedom to release the past and teach others how to find their relief, their freedom, their joy. Thank you for everything. And I'll see you in the next '57 on the road!

Momma, you were the best and the worst. LOL! You were the bestest mom ever growing up! Boy, did we do some damage! Chocolate bars, cooking, and Glendale Centre Theatre aside, did we ever have fun! Wow. But when it came to money, you didn't have a clue! You were my first pro bono client. If I knew then what I know now, I could have really helped you instead of doing it for you. Thank you for always believing in me. You never lost faith in me and always knew I could and would. Maybe you couldn't stand beside me, as you didn't always understand me, but you found a way to let me know you knew. Even after death, you found a way. You will always amaze me with your beauty, intelligence, determination, and fierce loyalty. Because of you, I am me. I love you!

Acknowledgments

I want to acknowledge my favoritist (yes, when you're an author, you can make up your own words!) people in the world, for without them, this book never would have been conceived, let alone written.

To My Knight in Shining Armor

To my awesome husband, Ron Cabourne. When I met you, I came alive. The sky was more blue, the grass more green, and the world became a better place. You make me want to be a better person. It's because of you that I'm driven to help the people I do. When I look into your beautiful blue eyes, I don't want to disappoint you. I'm driven to make you proud of me and of our life together as one. I promise we'll get that place in the Caribbean to offset the winters up North, and you can make all the furniture you want. It's a win-win, right? You're my knight in shining armor. Thank you for saving me! Thank you for always allowing me to be ME! Thank you for supporting us while I recuperated for over three years. Thank you for shouldering that burden alone. Thank you for learning to love a different wife, a new wife, a new life. Without your love, I'd be fractured. I'm forever yours! It's you, me, and Jesus — a 3-ply rope, together, forever!

To My Spiritual Community

Father Peter, you accepted me as I was, for who I was, am now, and am yet to be, at the time we met. I will always love and adore you for that. You brought me back to the church and helped me find my voice again so I could sing praises I hadn't sung in years. "River of Glory" is still my favorite hymn of joy. Thank you for making faith a simple thing!

Father Rich, you are my greatest mentor. I want to be you. You are a living example of what I believe God wants us to be, a humble living testimony of HIS love. When I see you, I hear one of the first Sunday school songs I ever learned start playing in my head,

> "This little light of mine, I'm gonna let it shine.
> This little light of mine, I'm gonna let it shine.
> This little light of mine, I'm gonna let it shine.
> Let it shine, let it shine, let it shine!"

Because of you, your transparency and willingness to show me your scars and frailties, I've learned to fight enough to win a few battles and publish this book. To quote another song, "It only takes a spark to get a fire going," and your spark got my fire going. Thank you! Thank you! Thank you for giving me the courage to find the worthiness within me to help others find the worthiness in themselves, and to persevere through it all.

Gentlemen, I love you so much. Thank you for grounding me in my spirituality again. You both are so humble that it's probably hard to receive this, so I'll just let God do the pouring of blessings onto you for me!

To My Medical Team

To my medical team, especially, Dr. Jeffrey Gross, Dr. Steven Eggelston, Atty, Dr. Amir Rafizad, Dr. Kenneth Wogensen, Dr. Karen Salter-Moss, Dr. Zenia Cortes, Dr. Jeanne Kim, Dr. David Wu, Dr. Richard Shubin, Dr. Jong Jeung, Dr. Heather MacDonald, and Jessica Uhl, P.A. ~ You all patched me up, along with all the physical therapists, nurses, aides, and interns. As I write this, it's four years ago that the accident happened. I never thought I'd get this far. Thank you for giving me my life back.

To the True to Intention Community

To Amanda Johnson, my beloved book coach and Messagepreneur™. Oh boy, tears! I love you so much. You've taken me from the wrong book project to this one, and then from a puddle of mush to success. Talk about transformation! And all I thought I was going to do was write a @#$%^&* book! LOL! There are no words to describe this journey, other than to say, "Phew! I'm glad that's over! Now let's start another!" See you for the next one!

And to the "Dare to Yes" Team, I humbly fall on my face with gratitude! Without you, I would not be *here*. Without that gentle, "No," I would, right now, be a professional volunteer. You all collectively saw this vision for me before I ever did. Thank you for holding the space for me until I was ready to step into it.

To My Coaches, Friends, and Team

To Ursula Mentjes. Without your business coaching, I'd still be wandering in circles believing "I couldn't." While always being a friend, it was the day in Dana Point when your coaching turned my life around. Thank you for all of the extra time you've spent with me to get me back in the zone and on fire again. The day I asked myself, "What would Ursula do now?", I knew I was on the right track. You've taught me how to push fear aside and do that thing that I fear most. Thank you. I don't think I'll ever be the same.

To LaVonne Shields. Girlfriend — You rock! Thank you for being the sounding board every entrepreneurial woman needs. From the suitcaseless business trip to the surf n' turf burgers to our book list, you're my girl! Thank you for allowing me to be your confidante and accountability buddy, and you, mine. My head would have exploded the first week of Synchronize if it weren't for YOU! A lot of what's been accomplished is attributable to our Power Calls! Power up, baby! We'll persevere together!

To Melissa Toppenberg. Okay, don't faint! Yes, without you, my dear, this book would not have gotten finished! You are extraordinary! And YOU pushed me to just do it! I've wanted to throw up more since hiring you than anyone else! You pushed me to do things I never thought I could. I am now a writing machine because of you. Thank you so much!

To Debbee Henry. You, my dearest, are the sister everyone wishes they could have. I'm so blessed to have you in my life. Without you, I would certainly have been alone much of the time. To say, "I love you," means very little. I am yours forever. I will always be there for you, forever. You are the best person on the planet. The most loving, selfless, generous, awesome, human being I know. I'm working my way up to you, babe! That's my retirement plan!

And to you, Stephanie Aceves, my sweet, intentional dancer, mommy, and student. Without your honest and vulnerable, impassioned plea to please write a step-by-step guide for you to follow after taking both of my classes (which were comprehensive and intense), this book would never have been conceived. This book really is for YOU.

To My Readers, Clients, and Community

To my awesome readers, clients, and community. It is for you that this story is told and this guide is written. If you know me, you know how I am. I genuinely care about you and want the best for you — YOU personally.

I hope and pray that this book will unlock the past if it has held you back, release you from its grip, and propel you into a future filled with promise, hope, and success. I value each and every one of you and pray that you all reach the goals and dreams you're all planning for.

With love and God's blessings,

Renée

Contents

Transforming Chaos into HarMoney

"Growth is an erratic forward movement:
Two steps forward, one step back.
Remember that and be very
gentle with yourself."
~ Julia Cameron ~

"But they that wait upon the LORD
shall renew their strength; they shall
mount up with wings as eagles;
they shall run, and not be weary;
and they shall walk, and not faint."
~ Isaiah 40: 31 ~

"He's turning," was the last thing I said, and then he plowed into me head-on, changing my life forever.

On September 25, 2009, at 7:55 a.m., I was on my way to pick up a girlfriend for a business breakfast. But by 8:00 p.m. that night, my future as a business owner, a wife, and a money savvy woman was in jeopardy.

- My car was totaled;
- I'd had two 1-hour conversations that I still have no recollection of;
- I'd been to the Emergency Room and back, and still have no clue how I got there;
- I'd lost my hearing due to an incredibly loud noise in my head; and
- I couldn't remember anything for longer than about ten seconds.

Within a month, my life became a series of daily doctors' appointments with neurologists, chiropractors, general practitioners, bone doctors, X-ray techs, and physical therapists.

I went from being a super overachiever, thriving as an extremely busy business owner of two businesses who served on several boards, to not realizing I was a businesswoman at all!

I'll never forget the day I remembered I owned a company and screamed to my husband, Ron, "I own a business! Where is it?" and he calmly replied, "It's downstairs where it's always been, Edith." He'd gotten in the habit of calling me "Edith Bunker," which I hated, even if I was completely out of it.

> I went from being a super overachiever, thriving as an extremely busy business owner of two businesses who served on several boards, to not realizing I was a business-woman at all!

She was a dingbat; I was brilliant. I knew I'd lost my way somehow since this accident, but it wasn't until more than two years later that it was confirmed I had too much in common with Edith.

We sat on a bench outside, and I gazed at the bougainvilleas, trying to get my head around what the doctor had just told to me. Finally, he nestled me under his arm, as it was time to get going. I kept putting one foot in front of the other as the cool breeze of the crisp March evening descended upon us. My head was spinning, and I clung to him for support while all the messages swirling around in my head bubbled to the top in one, blurted question.

"Did I just understand her to say that I'm brain injured?" I asked my husband as we began walking to the car.

Without looking at me or slowing our stride, he pulled me closer and murmured, "Yes." Twenty minutes earlier, after waiting more than a month for the results of my neuro-psyche evaluation, I'd listened to the doctor give us the test results and watched my husband crumble into tears before me. However, I didn't understand what was going on until that moment in the parking lot.

Turns out my brain had been on a 5-20 minute delay for several years, and I was just beginning to awaken to the reality of the situation.

At that moment, in the parking lot of Casa Colina, a center for rehabilitation for brain-injured patients, I wondered if my husband had been right.

Omg! I might just be Edith Bunker!

This news stole my hope and catalyzed a depression I'd never known before.

Total Impact

The head injury truly changed my personality. This change was apparent to everyone, including my business associates. I remember a few times where my new mantra became "Whatever!" and was at such a ridiculous level that my associates would say out loud for all to hear, "That's the accident talking, not Renée!" And I wouldn't even respond! Remember, twenty-minute delay!

I am not myself. Where did I go?

Being allergic to pain relievers and non-steroidal anti-inflammatory medications, I was also in a lot of pain most of the time, and with the head injury, I slept a lot. I went from sleeping five hours a night to fourteen hours a day!

> The head injury truly changed my personality.

When I was awake, I was more like a zombie than a human. My husband would say, "Let's go to the grocery store." I'd head upstairs to put some shoes on, and by the time I'd get there, I'd forget my mission, find my bedroom, see a magazine, crawl into bed, and start reading. Eventually, he'd come looking for me and, thoroughly irritated, would ask me what the heck I was doing.

I'd snap, "Reading, obviously!"

And he'd snap back, "Well, what happened to grocery shopping?"

I'd totally forgotten.

Needless to say, our relationship deteriorated, as I was more like a dependent child than the high-functioning adult he'd known. This went on for months until he was called away on business, and I was left alone for eight months to manage the house and everything in it.

I feel like a drain on the people around me. When will this end?

I'd lost my sense of order. There were times I'd forget things that we all take for granted, like changing out of my pajamas before leaving the house! When Ron was home, he'd catch me and ask, "You going to the store like that?" But when he was gone, I know I showed up a couple of times at my girlfriend's house in my pj's, thanks to her lovely daughter kindly asking, "Miss Renée, are those your pajamas?"

"Uh…yep! Guess my bump on the head got the best of me this morning! Thank God, it's you who caught me!" and I'd head back home.

> Now I couldn't subtract 7 from 100 twice without counting on my fingers.

If there was a real low point to being left alone, it was realizing that no one was paying the bills! I'd totally forgotten to pay them! Oh yeah. The electricity got shut off! Luckily, I was able to get it turned back on the same day, but I couldn't get the darn power back on myself and had to get the neighbor to help me with my "mushy" breaker switches. Talk about embarrassing!

I feel lost and humiliated. I can't even take care of myself...

As part of my cognitive therapy, my neurologist insisted that I get a job as a barista to learn numbers again because I couldn't do them anymore. Did I mention I used to be a financial advisor and a virtual walking computer? In fact, that was one of the things that caused my husband to fall in love with me — I caught him in a mathematical mistake and had the guts to tell him.

> And then the humiliation truly began. Being in finance, the industry had taken a hit in 2008, and as a result, my income had bottomed out with it.

Now I couldn't subtract 7 from 100 twice without counting on my fingers. I started working at Klatch Coffee near my home with a bunch of 20-somethings, which amounted to another blow to my ego and self-esteem. I couldn't hear the orders or remember them, I couldn't make change, and I had a full menu of drinks and food to remember with a staff of kids running circles around me.

Is this ever going to get better? Or is this the best I can hope for?

My team of doctors worked really hard to figure out the sources of my pain and hearing loss, and after fourteen months, they brought in a spinal surgeon because things weren't improving. After an injection procedure, my hearing was partially restored, but my pain was no better, and things escalated.

I wound up having half my neck replaced with a triple discectomy on September 1, 2011, followed by rotator cuff surgery on March 8, 2012. (Turns out my shoulder pain wasn't caused by my neck injury after all, but a huge rip in my shoulder!)

When will I be able to get back to my life? Could this get any worse?

And then the humiliation truly began.

Being in finance, the industry had taken a hit in 2008, and as a result, my income had bottomed out with it. With my health being challenged as it was, my income had been reduced to 25% of what it was in 2007, and I'd been struggling to pay my bills. I'd been hanging on this whole time, believing I would be getting better, but hadn't been, and so, in the beginning of 2012 — as I was sobbing in the parking lot of Casa Colina after getting my neuro-psyche results — I faced the reality that I was brain-injured and the possibility of me returning to my A+ personality was nil to none.

I'd been paying all along, and talking to my creditors, telling them I believed that I would be able to return to full-time work soon, but the interest rates were eating me alive and I knew that once I had the shoulder surgery, I would be on drugs and incapable of working.

I am a complete loser. I can't do this by myself.

I had to bite the bullet and address the elephant in the room. Being unable to handle things myself, I hired an attorney to help me go through the painful process of having to negotiate with my creditors and get out from under my bills due to my medical hardship. I was finally able to settle. The relief was worth it, but I wouldn't wish that process on my enemies.

I spent most of 2012 recovering from shoulder surgery, an incredibly painful experience. Comparing the two surgeries, the neck surgery was a cake walk including the 5-day hospital stay and the complication of a paralyzed right arm for fourteen weeks. To make matters worse, I was on heavy narcotic drugs that kept me in a near stupor for weeks. Never again!

Hope Emerges

In January 2013, I was granted a miracle and started hyperbaric oxygen treatments. It was during those forty treatments in that tube-like chamber that my life was truly returned to me. I remember how nervous I was during the very first treatment. Scared to go into the tube, I kept my eyes closed the whole time with my iPod playing music to keep me calm. But by the time it was over, I felt energized and invigorated. My sleep improved that night. I slept only nine hours, woke up refreshed without hitting the snooze button ten times, and felt more alert throughout the day. With every passing session, my acuity improved. It wasn't long before I wanted to live in that chamber. By the fortieth session, I was working with my tablet, phone, and laptop during the treatment, and my doctor was chuckling as I would knock on the glass and ask him to turn on my broadband so I could work.

The change in me was astounding…miraculous.

To this day, I still attend my Traumatic Brain Injury Group when I can so others can continue to have the hope that they, too, will recover in time.

What does this have to do with being a Money Savvy Woman?

I have worked with hundreds of women and professionals over the years, and there is one thing that is a constant:

Women who are not money savvy feel everything I felt while dealing with the fall-out of this accident...

- *Lost to themselves and their lives*
- *Like a drain on the people around them*
- *Powerless to change their circumstances*
- *Angry at whatever catalyzed the financial devastation*
- *Humiliated and looking for a way to hide the fall-out*
- *Desperate to feel like themselves again*
- *Scared to death it will never change*
- *Embarrassed to ask for help*

And, as I shared, I felt the same way about my financial circumstances...after years of being a Money Savvy Woman.

Stuff happens, right?

Accidents. Divorce. Unemployment. Tanking economies. Contracting businesses. Nightmare-health crises. Caregiving. Unexpected loss.

And before you continue reading, I want you to know that I see you. I feel your pain around the finances, and you are not alone.

> Women who are not money savvy feel everything I felt while dealing with the fall-out of this accident...

I started writing this book the year after my accident, and it has taken me almost three years to complete, but I didn't give up because I knew that you were out there, feeling lost, desperate, powerless, angry, humiliated, and scared.

And you don't have to be anymore.

Your current financial situation is the result of past circumstances, choices, and unhealthy mindsets about money that probably started when you were a child.

And today is a new day.

You may not be the same person you were before the financial hit happened, but that's okay too.

I'm not the same, never will be. My husband has accepted that his old wife is gone, and this new one is here to stay. We are closer now than ever before, and I love him for the sacrifices he made — like supporting us while I was on the Good Ship Lollipop!

> If I can come back from this nightmare and have it become the best thing that ever happened to me, you can learn to handle your money successfully. You can live in HarMoney™!

Multitasking is a thing of the past — don't try to call me while I drive. I'll either wind up ten miles past my destination or I won't hear a word you say!

But the good news is, I'm more focused and intentional than I've ever been in my life.

I love my life.

My purpose was made clear through this accident. Everything else was forcibly stripped away. I found out who my friends really were. Some were here for a season; some are here for a lifetime. I'm grateful for both.

The struggles you face might not be exactly like mine, but they're still struggles. You'll be stronger and wiser for them too as you move through them. I promise.

If I can come back from this nightmare and have it become the best thing that ever happened to me, you can learn to handle your money successfully. And I don't mean just handle it — I mean *use it to get what you want out of life. You can live in HarMoney™!*

You can get what you want – that monthly massage, that car, that new home, that vacation, or whatever else just popped into your head – and you probably don't have to make more money to do it. All you need is to develop your own rules, and your own style, and use the money to live *your* way…

In fact, at the beginning of every chapter, I share the story of purchasing a brooch I just had to have when I was in my early twenties, even though I didn't think I could afford it at first. But I did. I figured it out, and I'm going to show you how to get what you want too.

I will show you how, by sharing the most impactful money stories from my childhood, my single days, my first marriage, through my divorce, and then my second marriage. For those of you who are professionals and entrepreneurs, I also share the lessons I have learned as a businesswoman and entrepreneur.

I had to share the stories because the most important lesson I've learned along this journey toward living in HarMoney™, and helping others do the same, is this:

Most people need more than Money Basics to live in HarMoney^{TM}; they need to start at the beginning and figure out WHY the money isn't working.

More often than not, my clients have some painful money stories and messages from their childhood that have been driving their thoughts, feelings, and behaviors around money without them even knowing it.

> If you don't believe it yet, that's okay. I will hold that space for you.

Once we uncover those stories, we can begin to develop the other essentials: a healthy (healed) money mindset, steps to take and tools to implement them, and the self-compassionate determination to keep moving no matter what.

I've created this book to give you ALL of the above. By the end, you will have what you need to begin transforming your chaos into HarMoney™!

If you don't believe it yet, that's okay. I will hold that space for you. All you need to do is read this book, complete the Resetting Your Mindset exercises, and begin implementing the Tools for HarMoney™ as you go; and by the end, you will already begin to see results.

Take a deep breath. Remember, oxygen saved my life!

And let's do this!

Love and God's blessings,

Renée

9/25/2013

Chapter One

Where Did the HarMoney Go?

"Gratitude unlocks the fullness of life. It turns what
we have into enough, and more. It turns denial into
acceptance, chaos to order, confusion to clarity.
It can turn a meal into a feast,
a house into a home."
~ A Stranger ~

"This is the day which the LORD has made;
we will rejoice and be glad in it."
~ Psalms 118:24 ~

I was walking through a very fancy department store to get to a smorgasbord where I could eat lunch for $4 when it caught my eye. I looked at it for quite a while and walked away. I went back almost immediately, and then tried to walk away again, but came back and circled the case, several times.

Finally, the sales lady broke into my trance with a question, "Do you want to see it?"

I moved my eyes from the brooch to her face and looked at her blankly, stunned. There she was — impeccably dressed in her beige, Channel-styled suit. She was just like the brooch — too rich for my blood. Yet, her eyes told me another story. They were soft, kind, and inviting.

I'd been tracking my money carefully and knew this beauty would wipe out my paycheck, which just happened to be burning in my hands. I knew I had no business being there.

I should be going to lunch and getting three vegetable side dishes for 99¢ each!

But I couldn't move. I was frozen…

Disappearing Dimes

"Shhhh!" I whispered through the doors of the closet. "They're coming!" I could hear my little sister giggling as she crouched, waiting in the dark.

In walked a very short line of our neighborhood girlfriends, all six of them, ages five to eight. They were coming to see my sister, otherwise known as the Carol Burnett of our generation, perform a show in our closet.

As soon as they were all seated, I flung wide the closet door. There was Denise, with a huge smile on her face, tap dancing her heart out on the wooden floor, for all of our friends to watch. She followed the dance with a joke or two, then another dance, and then I slammed the door shut. We rolled on the floor with laughter and, at the end, collected a dime from each one of our patrons.

We weren't in the business of making money back then. We were in the business of having fun. Every few days or weeks, we'd put on a show and collect the money. And since I never really thought of what to do with the money, I just threw the few coins in my top dresser drawer and forgot about them until I wanted to buy a candy bar at Ted's Liquor. And then I was shocked.

Where did my money go?!?

I rummaged through the contents of the drawer, looking for even one dime, and slammed it with frustration when I realized what had happened. *Someone has stolen my money! How much was in there anyway?*

Being the industrious child I was, I found a few other ways to make money since Denise would only do so many shows in a closet, and our friends weren't going to pay for what she did for free. (My first lesson in business: Always have a back-up plan). My back-up plans consisted of collecting carts and bringing them in from the parking lot for the local grocer, running the occasional errand for a mom at work, riding my bike to a stereo store to clean, and even mounting EKGs for a doctor once I proved I knew what I was doing. I made some really great money back in those days, especially for a 10-year-old, but I threw all the money in my top dresser drawer. And what do you know? The same thing happened again and again. The money disappeared.

Where is your money doing the disappearing act?

The Value of Tracking Money

As a child, I never gave the loss of my money much thought beyond the initial frustration of not being able to buy my candy bar. I seriously doubt Denise had anything to do with it. She had a direct connection to the deep pockets in our family, also known as my dad. I honestly don't know who took my money, and it doesn't matter. The point is that this was my first experience with money, and I didn't have any training on the basics of money — tracking income and keeping it safe. No one had taught me. For some reason in my parents' eyes, it wasn't important.

Because I wasn't aware of my income, I didn't learn to value my money, even though I was really good at making it. I also had no way to know how much I'd lost. I couldn't turn around and say, "Hey, I'm missing 50 cents" or "I'm missing $50." Nor could I say, "Hey, I'm up 50 cents or $50." I was just a kid who didn't know anything...but it didn't have to be that way.

I really wish that someone had taught me those basics then. They could have saved me years of asking myself the question, "Where did the money go?" and the pain of having to learn it the hard way, many years later in my adulthood.

When did the first "magic" money
disappearing act occur in your life?

Where has all the
money gone, long time passing?

Do you remember that song, "Where have all the flowers gone…long time passing?" That may as well have been the theme song for the first two years of my second marriage. When my second husband, Ron, and I got married at thirty-seven years old, we figured that at that age we had money figured out and chose to keep our money separate. While basking in the glow of our honeymoon and first year of being married, we let everything slide, including our finances. In fact, we let everything slide through the second year, too.

We went on an expensive honeymoon, ate out a lot, were very generous with gift-giving, etc. I bought my husband a new wardrobe, including shoes. (He only wore jeans and a t-shirt for formal occasions — you know the type.) We turned forty and that required a domestic holiday with family, a Caribbean dive vacation to visit

> They could have saved me years of asking myself the question, "Where did the money go?" and the pain of having to learn it the hard way, many years later in my adulthood.

friends, and a party. We had any excuse to spend money for any occasion. We were out of control.

> By the time we woke up to what we were doing financially, we realized that we were essentially spending our emergency and retirement funds!

Until one morning I heard him scream "Hey!" from the office.

"What?" I hollered back from the living room.

"Where's our savings?" he shouted, half accusatory and half wondering, from the wooden captain's chair at his desk.

"What do you mean? Was I in charge of saving savings?" I asked with a snarky attitude as I leaned in the doorway. "I put my money in at work."

With annoyance dripping off every word, he made his declaration. "I'm not talking about retirement. I'm talking about *our* money. I haven't saved *a cent* since day one. I've been treating you...us...to a party! Are you aware of that?"

By the time we woke up to what we were doing financially, we realized that we were essentially spending our emergency and retirement funds! This realization did not come easily to either of us. Both of us are very strong-willed individuals. We were both successful at our jobs. We both had our way of doing things, and neither of us was ready to concede to the other. Money soon became an "issue." The minute the word came up, it was an argument. Neither of us had a clue as to where our money was going, nor did we have any idea how to talk about it constructively. As long as we never spoke about money, we were in bliss. You've heard that phrase, "ignorance is bliss." Well, we'd been living in ignorance, and the resentment was eating away at our marriage.

One day, a friend called me to share that she had changed jobs and needed some training. "Could I come over and practice with the two of you?" She told us she would be able to tell us our retirement date, and we thought that was interesting. We didn't really know what we were getting into, but we just wanted to help her, so we said, "Yes."

Our lives changed that day.

When she arrived that afternoon, we all gathered around our dining room table, shared some tea, and caught up with each other for a bit. Eventually, she dug into her questionnaire and cut to the chase.

"What do you want in your life?" she asked.

"Uh, what do you mean, 'what do I want in my life?'" my husband kidded. "I want to build elevators until retirement. Then I want to build furniture."

I tried to digest the question myself. "I've never really thought about it before."

Ron and I looked at each other with blank expressions. "What do you think?" I asked.

"I don't know. What do you think?" he responded. Suddenly, the image of the indecisive vultures from *Jungle Book* came flooding back into my mind.

"We never really thought about it." I said, feeling a bit sheepish.

She told us that we were essentially trying to drive to New York without a map if we didn't have a clue what we wanted to do with our money. Both of us were stunned.

"What?" Ron asked. "We're saving for retirement at our jobs. Isn't that what we're supposed to be doing?

"*When* do you want to retire?" she asked.

"Huh? You mean we have a choice?" he responded with a tone that matched my own surprise.

"Of course you have a choice!" she said with the biggest smile I'd ever seen. She knew she was imparting the most fabulous information in the world. "You can choose when you want to retire, where you want to live, how you want to live, and with whom! It's all up to you! You just have to decide and then plan it! It's all in here." She pointed to the questionnaire.

At the end of our meeting, we agreed we needed to track our money to see where all of it was going, and maybe find some to put away for our future.

We decided to track the money for a month, and then talk about our findings. And we made up a set of rules for that discussion too: No yelling. No screaming. No shaming...

What my husband and I discovered proved to be a life-changing awakening.

After tracking every expense for only seven days, I had learned all I needed to know about my spending. I knew what changes I had to make. I wasn't as out of control as I thought. I was just making large expenditures in all the wrong places...one in particular.

So I gathered my courage that night and, when the timing was right, said to my husband, "I think I need to talk about the money thing. I don't know about you, but I've already learned a lot."

Surprisingly, he said, "Me too."

So there we sat at the kitchen table, saying nothing for what seemed like eternity. Finally, I figured since I was the one who came up with the bright idea to talk three

After tracking every expense for only seven days, I had learned all I needed to know about my spending. I knew what changes I had to make.

weeks early, I would go first. I took a big gulp and blurted out, "I'm spending $25 a week at Starbucks!"

I refused to look at him. I thought for sure he was going to yell at me.

Why isn't he saying anything?

I had a boss at the time who I felt was torturing me, and every morning at 6:45, I would walk into Starbucks and order my $4.25 coffee drink, and because I was so generous, I threw the $.75 into the tip jar. And if it was a really heinous day, I'd do it twice, just because I deserved it for putting up with so much nonsense. So you can see how I was easily spending $25 a week, if not more.

Waiting for his response was like waiting an eternity. Finally, I heard a little voice, barely above a whisper...

"I'm spending $32 a week at McDonald's®," he confessed, sagging into the kitchen chair, with his head hanging low, looking as defeated as he sounded.

"WHAT?!?" I practically screamed. Here I thought for sure he was going to yell at me, and I had turned the tables on him. I was doing the yelling (and breaking the rules).

"We don't need junk food! What are you doing eating at McDonald's®?"

"After work, I'm hungry. I go through the drive-thru and order a large fry and a shake, and I supersize it!" he blurted out as the guilt oozed off him.

You can only imagine the conversation that followed. After wrangling through issues of weight gain and money flying senselessly out the window, we looked at each other and immediately realized that we had this thing licked.

Off the top of your head, where are you spending unnecessary money?

Here's what we did:

- I quit going to Starbucks. I bought a five pound bag of Starbucks beans at a warehouse store and a milk frother for $8. I took a French press and the frother to work and made my own lattes daily, saving myself a small fortune.

- My hubby went to the local Trader Joe's and bought a bunch of yummy snack foods that were both healthy and portable, so that he could eat them after work on the ride home instead of being tempted to drive through McDonald's®.

- We both saved all of our change from cash expenditures in a collection of cigar boxes. When one filled up, we started another. It was exciting to see them stack up like little bricks in our money-savings wall in the hallway cabinet.

The result:

In just thirteen months, we were on our way to our reward: a PRE-PAID 8-Day, 7-Night DIVE TRIP. Oh my gosh, it was amazing to have the "extra" money to do that!

If we can do it, you can do it too.

If you're single, this step is a piece of cake.

"Oh, I have to track it in my business too?"

The day my friend came to help us plan for our future changed my life, not only with regards to our personal finances but also in my career.

As she asked us the questions about our future, I could feel my excitement mounting, but not just for our personal finances. Pictures of my childhood dream of helping people just like she was helping me began to flash through my mind, so much so that I had to really focus to stay in the conversation.

What is this job? Can I do it too? I wanna do this! I wanna do this! I wanna do this!

Finally, I stopped her midsentence and asked, "How did you get this job? Can I do it too?"

I had just found my dream career!

Immediately, I went to work on obtaining the proper licensing so I could work in the insurance and investment industry. Being the Type A personality that I am, I was successful rather quickly. By the end of 2000, I had all of the licensing necessary to work as a personal financial consultant.

As exciting as all this success was, I didn't realize I was getting involved in a multi-level marketing company and what that actually meant. It required a lot of sales meetings and rallies on top of my full-time job, and I wasn't exactly prepared for the additional cost of gasoline, the eating out because I was never home and, in hindsight, the low pay.

I was truly in love with this career. I was good at it. My name was at the top of a lot of the leader boards. I had a lot of trophies.

But I missed a lot of family events (which to this day I regret), and I never seemed to make any money beyond being able to pay my expenses. It seemed my checks evaporated before I ever received them.

What would it feel like to keep some of your money?

Again I began asking myself, "Where is all the money going?"

What I'd begun to practice in my personal life with my husband, I hadn't yet applied to my business. I didn't have a clue as to where my money was coming from or where it was going.

Don't get me wrong. I knew it was coming in from the business, but which revenue stream? Life insurance sales? Securities sales? Home mortgage refinancings? It would have been helpful to know where my strength was and then capitalize on that.

The most painful part, however, was the outflows. Where was it all going?

When I finally started paying attention, and decided to answer this question by tracking it, I realized pretty quickly that I was spending too much on gas, driving all over creation to my sales meetings (120 miles round trip);

and as a leader, I was making that trip at least three times a week. If I had tracked those expenses early on, I could have made some adjustments, such as planning meetings along that route to save me time, fuel, and wear and tear on my car. But I didn't, and it cost me in more ways than money.

When I looked at the food costs – networking meetings, meals on-the-go, and taking clients out — it added up to a tremendous amount of money. Mistakenly, I thought I could just "write it off." True, but not how I thought. To be clear, you must be 50 miles from your home for the convenient food-on-the-go to be written off; and even then, it's only 50% of the cost. But still, it all added up and undercut my profit! Did I really want to eat my profit? No, I didn't.

In business, I've learned the hard way that it's all about delivering 5-star quality while being as efficient as possible in relation to our expenses. We must know what those are if we plan to keep them as low as possible while still delivering our top-notch product or service.

Resetting Your Mindset:
The Tracking Conversation

Most women (and men) come to me when they are at the end of their financial (and emotional) rope. The pain of not knowing how to track, manage, and save their money has resulted in one or more of the following: lots of debt, no savings, and the feeling of being a victim to their money while living paycheck to paycheck.

Instead of staying focused on everything you don't have, focus on what you do have.

I completely understand the "end of the rope" feeling, and yet before you actually start working on your financial plan by tracking the money, I want to encourage you to start from a different place emotionally.

Instead of staying focused on everything you don't have, focus on what you do have. Sure, you may not have that vacation home you wanted, or a cushion for retirement, but if you have a roof over your head and a full tummy, you have something to be grateful for.

And that's how we move from the mindset of scarcity to one of abundance...by focusing on what we do have and feeling truly and deeply grateful for it.

I Am Grateful

Make a list of everything you have to be thankful for right now. Start the habit of closing each day with a simple list of five (5) things you're grateful for that day. Graciousness has a way of creating abundance. You'll be amazed at how living in gratitude opens doors to abundance.

Tools for HarMoney™: *Track Your Money with the Dollars to $ense Audit*

It's a very simple process. Here are the rules:

1. For one full month, track your income and your expenses…all of them! From the largest to the smallest of expenditures, you need to know where your money is going. Use a 3 x 5 spiral bound memo pad to do it! Easy! Or you can download and print a support tool at: www.MoneySavvyWoman.com/tools-registration.

2. If you are a couple, after the time period is up, set a time when you will have a discussion about what you have each recorded. Let me emphasize — this is a discussion.

   a. No raising of the voices.

   b. No being defensive.

   c. No domineering the conversation.

   d. No alcohol, candles, or dinner.

3. Take notes during this conversation as to what worked and what did not work for the month.

4. Make a game plan as to what changes you will put in play to make a difference in next month's bottom line.

5. Set a time to review your progress towards next month's goal, preferably 1-2 weeks from this time.

Remember, you're on the same team. You're working together.

And if you are single, what would be more important than showing yourself a little love, compassion and understanding as you embark on your journey to HarMoney?

Additionally, if you have a setback, immediately forgive yourself and move on. It's not the end of the world. Creating healthy money muscles will take some time.

Give yourself credit for getting on the path to money savviness!

Chapter Two

Redefining HarMoney

"Our past is a story existing only in our minds.
Look, analyze, understand, and forgive.
Then, as quickly as possible, chuck it."
~ Marianne Williamson ~

"Therefore if any man be in Christ, he is a new creature: old things are passed away; behold, all things are become new."
~ 2 Corinthians 5:17 ~

I gulped as she retrieved the brooch, leaned over the glass case, pinned it to me, and handed me a mirror.

My heart almost leapt out of my chest. I never wanted any "thing" more in my life than this silly piece of metal with its lovely purple quartz stone and iridescent crystals. It lit up the room once freed from the case.

I knew if I could only wear that brooch, it would become my power symbol, lifting me up whenever my insecurities threatened to sabotage me.

I had always loved fashion, but this was a new level. My clothes, my style, my hair and makeup, together, created a package that made a statement: "I have it going on." But that statement was more for those who saw me, and this silly piece of jewelry somehow spoke to *ME!* It shouted to me, *I have it going on!*

I knew if I could only wear that brooch, it would become my power symbol, lifting me up whenever my insecurities threatened to sabotage me. Wearing it, I could walk on water if I had to!

My Library Bank

We were just getting ready to sit down to dinner when the phone rang. My mother wiped her hands on the towel and dashed for the phone on the wall. "Yes," I heard her say, and then she flashed me a look. A pit formed in my stomach, and it had nothing to do with the fact that I was hungry. She hung up the phone and said, "Renée, that was the librarian at the North Hollywood library. She found some money in the book you returned today."

"Oh, geez!" I jumped up. "That's my babysitting money!"

"Well, you'll have to go by tomorrow to get it. Her name is Kathy," she said as she put the casserole on the table. "You need to learn to be more careful with your money. It's a good thing your father isn't home yet to hear this!"

> "You need to learn to be more careful with your money. It's a good thing your father isn't home yet to hear this!"

Kathy knew me too well. Often, she would chastise me for talking too loudly inside the library when my class would visit, or for trying to take too many books out, or for returning my books with money inside, as I'd done before. I was lucky to have Kathy be the one in charge of that task that particular day. She was nice, but firm. I was relieved that I would get my money back, but a little scared to have to face her.

The next day, after school, I ran across the busy street to the library. Entering the dark, quiet building, I stopped dead in my tracks. For one, my eyes had to adjust to the inside light, and two, there's no running in libraries. I had to calm down and find my "indoor" voice over my beating heart.

Once I made the turn to the customer counter, there she was, in her blue dress and cream-colored sweater, surveying the books stacked all around her at the check-in counter. Oh boy. I could feel the sweat collecting on my forehead. "Hello. My name is Renée Riedel. I…"

Glancing through her wire-framed glasses at me, she reached for an envelope with my name on it. She smiled and leaned over the counter with the envelope to whisper, "Hard worker, you are. Find a safer place for your money, Miss Riedel!"

"Yes, Ma'am," I murmured, and sheepishly took my money, walked as slowly as I could without running to the door, and then ran across the street back to where I was supposed to be — in front of the school with my two little sisters.

Instead of throwing my money into my top drawer where it would surely disappear, I had begun to collect it in the book I was reading…which was from the library. I would babysit several times a week and collect the bills in the book, often using them as the bookmark or during the week as change drawer for my clients. Often, I would move the cash to the front of the book and forget it was there, and then when the time came, return the book to the library. (I had a lot going on in school, okay? Honest!)

Where are the "silly" places you have left your money and regretted it?

My mother got that call once a month for a few months. It was embarrassing — and I was SUPER lucky to have such an honest librarian make those calls.

I wanted to be fashionable and to keep up with my more affluent friends. I was learning very quickly that money was the answer to the majority of these needs.

The first three times, I had to go into the library, pick up my money after school, and face the librarians myself which became more and more difficult. But the fourth time, my mother had to go so they could lecture her.

Up until that point, I didn't quite get why it mattered, but I was beginning to. Again, when I was just a kid, it was fun to make money and spend it on candy, toys, and stuff. I was older now. Things were beginning to change. I didn't just want those "kid" things; I wanted to be fashionable and to keep up with my more affluent friends. I was learning very quickly that money was the answer to the majority of these needs.

As a kid, no one taught me how to reconcile my personal values with my money aspirations. Money was nothing more to me than a bookmark! Through my experience, I came to believe that my money had to be spent quickly or it disappeared — literally — as the top drawer abyss and the library zone proved. No one told me that "money was a tool to achieve my goals based on my values," in a language I understood. My mom had tried. I just didn't get it.

But as I look back, I did have a clear set of values driving my spending, even if I didn't know it at the time.

Purchase	Value
Clothes:	I liked fashion and helped my parents out by buying some of my own clothes.
Books:	I loved reading, especially Nancy Drew Mysteries…getting paid to go on an adventure while kids slept seemed too good to be true.
Fun:	Youth Night, movies, makeup, and anything else my dad could otherwise have the power to say I couldn't go to if I didn't have the money.

I began to learn that money, in some cases, meant power. Those who had it could get things. It was clear that I valued the freedom to be able to join my friends in their wardrobe choices and activities, like every other teenaged girl.

What did you believe money could get you when you were young?

Misunderstanding "The Usual"

Nearly every Friday night, my husband and I go to "our joint." One night as we walked into the restaurant, Ron asked, "Is that a new outfit?"

"Yes, I bought it because it's comfortable and was on sale." I responded knowing that the downward spiral was about to begin and we hadn't even ordered yet.

Please don't let this ruin the night before it begins, I silently prayed.

"You guys gonna have the usual?" the waiter interrupted, as he seated us. He knows...it's generally the same thing, at the same table, every Friday.

My husband glared at me. I nodded. He glanced up at our waiter. "Yep. The usual..."

He turned back to me. "I'm telling you, all you do is spend, spend, spend! When does 'saving' ever come into your equation?" he hissed at me.

"Well, I don't see you doing anything different! We come here every week and you order a $32 steak, the most expensive thing on the menu. Why's that?" I shot back under my breath.

"I happen to like steak, and I work hard! If I want to eat a freakin' steak, I'm going to eat a freakin' steak!" he barked.

"My bloody dress doesn't cost that much, and I'm not buying one of these a month! Why am I always the one that gets blamed for not saving? You can start any time you want to!" I cajoled.

"I'm telling you, all you do is spend, spend, spend! When does 'saving' ever come into your equation?" he hissed at me.

"Like it's going to make a difference."

This, he said, in total defeat. He looked out across the table with detached, blank eyes. The mood was set. I wondered if he really believed that saving money doesn't make a difference, or if he was just being argumentative.

"That's not true. It can make a difference. It has to. How can we ever have a future? We have to try or we're doomed." I said just as much to myself as I did to him. And there was no response. It seemed that our financial future would die a certain death.

And there it was...our main dilemma. We had different values. He didn't value my new outfit. I didn't value ordering the most expensive steak on the menu because we could. Based on that, we didn't trust how the other spent our money, which spilled over into other arenas of the unknown.

How does this argument usually unfold in your relationship, or in your own head?

If you have had an argument — or lots of arguments — like this, all hope is not lost!

Ron and I are very strong individuals who are stubborn, as well. Our challenges were just like many of yours; we had different styles of communication and different experiences that brought us to where we currently were.

For a long time, conversations with my husband over money were very difficult. We couldn't say the word "money" without tension. We couldn't even see hope in a plan together. That was the terrifying part; he just wasn't the planning type. I lived and breathed this stuff, but for him, it was completely foreign and didn't seem logical to plan something so far into the future that may not actually happen.

We needed to get onto the same page financially. The Dollars-to-Sense Audit had told us *how* we were spending our money, but not much else. We'd had the "finger-pointing" conversation so many times, it wasn't *like* a broken record, it *was* a broken record. But this time, it came like a smack in the face, as I felt we hadn't really learned anything. It was getting us nowhere fast, except perhaps divorce court.

And the fact was, I loved my husband and he loved me. Love was not our problem. *This* conversation, or lack thereof, was the problem, as well as the behaviors underlying it.

> We'd had the "finger-pointing" conversation so many times, it wasn't like a broken record, it was a broken record. It was getting us nowhere fast, except perhaps divorce court.

This financial conversation can be, and is often riddled with "guilt." Breaking free of this emotion gives you and your money energy — life — it never had before. Giving this energy direction is a necessary step in achieving your success.

In Chapter 1, you witnessed a conversation between my husband and me, much akin to this one, which led to the Dollars and Sense Audit when we realized that we were spending a lot of money on things that we didn't value at all.

But *this* conversation also included something about what we couldn't decide was more "valuable" — clothing for a promotion or dinner out when exhausted versus saving money. All of a sudden, *values* became the topic.

For a couple of years, we had been dragging each other through the mud, saying truly hurtful things toward each other because we didn't stop to ask one simple question, "Why do you VALUE spending money on that?"

When Ron and I made a list of our values, individual and joint, we were excited to find the core values that would serve as a strong foundation for our financial planning.

We valued our *Faith* first and foremost as the foundation of both our marriage and our finances. We knew that slapping on a harness wasn't going to be easy and that our lives had to change or nothing was going to change financially. We just couldn't change a little in one area and expect savings to grow and the mortgage to reduce to the degree we wanted. Both of us wanted big change. It took a lot of work, and so we decided to pull from a higher source and put our faith at the top of the list. By doing that, we could pray for strength to make sound decisions with our money. We both feel it gave us the added energy we needed to "straighten up and fly right" when we might have chosen to throw in the towel and indulge in something that we might have regretted later.

We valued our *Marriage* very much, so that was the second most important value. We knew we had to communicate better. We had to learn to value growing up differently and respecting each other's individualism. We agreed it wasn't fair to throw guilt over tools in the garage and new outfits at each other anymore. We were a team.

As for our *Health*, we valued improving it and made the correlation between fresh food and better bottom lines, physically and financially.

We both valued a better *Financial Future*. That's what all this fuss was about. We just didn't know how to go about it together while having Fun. Was that possible? As kids, we only knew of disappointment and strife by witnessing our parents struggle with their finances. Knowing what we valued as a couple, we couldn't remain stubborn, mean, and unforgiving if we were truly going to meet our goal of staying together as a couple and having a sound financial future.

If you have a partner, can you guess their top 3 values?

But there was more discovery ahead of us as we began to plan and spend according to those values.

It was several months before the next level showed up through a conflict over our Friday night out spending.

"You value the fruits of your labors? Who doesn't?" I asked with a tone that said, *"You need to explain that to me."*

"Yeah. Like when we go out on Friday nights, that steak is my reward for putting up with all the crap at work. Yeah, I know it pisses you off, but I look forward to it every week."

For some reason, at that moment, I finally heard him and it all clicked into place. I finally got it.

Even though our values were the same when we talked about them and made the list, we didn't go deep enough in our conversation to discover that while we both truly valued taking a break from going out on our date night every Friday night, there were still a few important differences between us.

I didn't get that when it comes to food and dining out, my husband was willing to pay any amount of money to *Feel Good*. That's what mattered to him. He just wanted to eat whatever came most highly recommended or looked the most mouth-watering on the menu. The price didn't matter. What mattered was what appealed to him in that moment and made him and his tummy feel good. I, on the other hand, was a creature of habit and could eat the same salad over and over. Same value, yet different experience for each of us when it came to menu options.

When it came to valuing the actual break of the Friday night out, I valued *Being Served*, including all of the interaction with the servers. It was, for me, what made the whole going out for dinner worth it. So if we went to a fine dining spot or a hole-in-the-wall joint, we had better go where I liked the people and the service was good. I wanted an experience of socializing, which my husband couldn't have cared less about.

Even though our values were the same when we talked about them and made the list, we didn't go deep enough in our conversation to discover that there were still a few important differences between us.

The result of these deeper conflicting values? He would gobble up his delicious meal and then be ready to trot out the door while I was barely through my side salad. Often, he'd impatiently hurry me through my meal so we could go back home. Friction ensued more often than not until we figured out our values in this area.

Now that we know what's most important to us, we ask the all-important questions before heading out the door:

- Are we on a limited budget? If so, where can we go where we can't break the bank? Sometimes it's the taco or hamburger joint.

- Are we in the mood to be able to kick back and relax? If not now, when can we so I get that feeling at some point this weekend? And what are we going to do now so I don't jump out of my skin, as I was expecting that to take place until five minutes ago?

Once this light went on for us and we started asking these questions, the ruffled feathers smoothed out rather quickly.

When it came to other expenditures, we were able to look at our finances differently when we asked ourselves this question: "Does buying this   (fill in the blank)   support our values of [this, that, and the other?]" It really gave direction to our out-of-control behavior in the beginning — when slapping on a harness was the hardest.

Suddenly, a new sense of life entered our relationship. We were committed to our relationship, willing to do the work necessary to create a better and stronger future for ourselves, and things began to pop — in more ways than one!

We had to be willing to find out what the backstory was, what the driving force was, or "the why," without being ready to pounce. Realizing what made each other tick was a huge step forward in knowing what actions to take and which ones to drop. We stopped before spending and thought of each other before acting, specifically, spending away from each other's values. We'd come home and report to each other how we didn't spend money that day on coffee or food, and how we enjoyed the experience. Shopping for a dress actually became more fun as I'd take him with me. I'd make it "us" time. He always enjoyed the "scenery," while I was confident he would see I wasn't

By focusing on what values we shared, making that our strength together, it reignited our passion of togetherness.

out to break the bank. There were times he even chose a more expensive dress because it looked better and was better quality.

We were taking action, reaching our goals. But more importantly, we were building trust in each other financially. *It felt good.* And over the years, we've grown to trust each other.

And it all started when we took the time to ask *Why?* and began identifying the common values that now keep our financial focus clear.

We were able to connect meaning to the action of spending money that directly related to the resulting outcome or balance. The energy brought an excitement and enthusiasm to our marriage that in many cases surpassed the uneasiness or awkwardness of our shortcomings. By focusing on what values we shared, making that our strength together, it reignited our passion of togetherness, and this flowed over into other aspects of our marriage, including intimacy.

What other areas of your life are being affected by the financial stress?

Through this process of aligning our values, we had become a team.

It takes courage to implement changes. Whether you're single or in a relationship, someone has to step up to the plate to reel in reality, and this can be tough. No one wants to be the bad guy. On the other hand, it takes courage to change. And then, it takes courage to affirm it and create a new habit.

It also takes a while to integrate the learning across other areas of our lives.

And I'm Doing This Because...?

You know my career story. I fell in love with this career when trying to find answers to my own financial questions. I hit the ground running like a dried up sponge, seeking information, scouring up everything I could find both personally and professionally. I already shared that I knew I didn't want to be in a multi-level company pretty early on, but it did take me a while to figure out what MY professional values were.

When I became a Certified Financial Planner® (CFP®) in January 2008, I was finally given permission to play the game I had always been playing, but on my terms. I swore to a Code of Ethics, and was very proud to serve in that manner. It was during that process that I realized how different my values were from what I had actually been doing the previous seven years and began the seedling of something different.

Initially, my values were pretty basic: if you have a need for financial services, I'm here to fill that need. I didn't really ask any questions. I needed the money. I still put my clients' needs first in whatever they needed, but I was all over the place in what I offered. For example, I worked for an elite, high-end, boutique Broker-Dealer who would often tell me what they were focused on, and as a result, what I should be focused on. At one point, I was selling life insurance, three different types of annuities, mutual funds, stocks, bonds, an IPO that my broker-dealer was the main dealer of, several high-risk alternative products, long-term care insurance, and disability insurance. It was exhausting!

At the end of 2008, I left my broker/dealer and Registered Investment Advisor (RIA) of over six years and struck out on my own. I had found the courage to get behind my own values of truth, integrity, and financial literacy to launch my own RIA and offer wealth management and coaching with literacy as the foundation without having to deal with that one statement on the "new account" securities application every client had to sign, which essentially read, "I may not do what is in your best interest as my loyalty is with my broker-dealer." As a full-disclosure girl, I had to point that statement out to each and every client. I hated it. I was honest and ethical, yet this statement implied that I may not do what is in their best interest — and it was true while I was working for someone else. I could only offer what my broker-dealer allowed me to offer.

Now, on my own, free of the general securities license, I could truly put my clients' needs first. I could seek out whatever they needed, find it, and get it for them. If I didn't want to offer it myself, I could bring in someone else who did without "selling away" hanging over my head.

What an awesome feeling it was to be completely independent. I soared over the moon. I was in the lap of luxury. The world was my oyster. So, so, sooooo happy... for about a year, and then I realized my true professional values were still a smidge out of balance.

Even though I had dropped my general securities license,

I was still following the direction of all the voices of my well-intentioned mentors, "Sell. Sell. Sell." When I finally listened to my own voice, I heard a very clear message, "Educate your people, Renée. They need to know!"

This was the beginning, the seed of Money Savvy Woman, the financial literacy and coaching component of my work with people desperate for answers.

> Until my values were in line with my money, my goals for my relationship, and my career, I couldn't get anything to happen.

Until my values were in line with my money, my goals for my relationship, and my career, I couldn't get anything to happen. And it all started with asking myself, *Why?* and communicating my answers to those questions to the people around me. It was a valuable lesson to learn…pun intended!

Resetting Your Mindset:
The Values Conversation

We've done a lot of talking about discovering what is valuable to us. It's important to know what you like and what you don't, what you "value" spending your money on and what you won't. It isn't enough to simply say, "I know." One needs clarity.

Clarity makes the difference of getting what you want or settling for a "version" of what you want.

> You have to be free to give yourself a fresh start, and by a fresh start, I mean a clean slate.

Having that clarity is an essential piece in breathing new life into your current one. It takes courage to look inside (and dare to share, if you're a couple).

Once you begin to track your expenses, you may feel a little shocked at how much you have been spending on items or experiences that aren't really in alignment with your values. I see it over and over again with my clients. They track for a month and come back to me wide-eyed. So the first exercise I have to take them through to reset their mindset is around Forgiveness.

Forgive yourself for all of your past financial mistakes.

And, if you don't think you're worthy of forgiveness – yes, you are! Everyone is worthy of forgiveness. You are here on this planet to enjoy your life, to live your life to the fullest, and to live the purpose of your existence. So get over those past mistakes. They're done with. That's it.

Forgive yourself for whatever is holding you back.
Forgive yourself for overdrawing your checking account.
Forgive yourself for overspending.
Forgive yourself for living beyond your means.
Forgive yourself for all your past credit card debt.
Forgive yourself for your impulse buying.
Forgive yourself for whatever you need to forgive yourself for...and then be done with it.

You have to be free to give yourself a fresh start, and by a fresh start, I mean a clean slate. Picture a nice clean white board in front of you with nothing on it, not even a trace of what was there before hand. That's the type of forgiveness I'm talking about right now.

I Am Forgiving

Forgive yourself for your mistakes. Stop yourself from beating yourself up. Think of yourself as your own child. Would you say those things to your own kid? You need to forgive yourself and move on.

Remember the saying, "Don't look back. You're not going in that direction anymore!" You have the power to catch yourself and turn it all around.

Repeat the following line and fill in the blank as many times as you need until you cannot think of another thing to forgive yourself for.

I forgive myself for _____.

Clearing your mind of all anger, regrets, and fears, again, forgiving others and yourself, so you can move on, frees you of all negative self-talk, thinking, and "programming,"

Tools for HarMoney™:
Identify & Share Your Values

Alright! Now that you have forgiven yourself (or started to!), it's time to clearly define those values.

Whether you are doing this for yourself alone, or with your partner, this process will be very enlightening and give you a sense of immediate relief and freedom around money.

If you are doing this with your significant other, the process will feel a little more complicated, but it isn't if you approach it affirming your love for each other and your desire to be powerful partners in creating your financial future.

In this process, you will discover the differences in your money personalities. You MUST respect these differences. You cannot use them against each other later. Discovering the differences enables you to build up your strengths, minimize your weaknesses, and create a solid foundation to build upon financially.

Values Exercise

First, review the list and underline the values that resonate YES when you read them. The first time I did this, I underlined roughly 20 of these values.

Next, go back and look at your list and whittle it down to your Top 10 by:

1. Identifying the repetition and reducing two or three answers to just one. For instance, if you underlined Confidence and Composure, and in your mind, those two values represent the same idea, then choose one, circle it, and cross out the other.

2. If you've still got too many on your list, look at two of them at a time and work your way down the list, asking the question, "If I had to choose between these two, which one would I choose?" Circle the ones that you choose over the others until you get to your Top 10.

Once you have your Top 10, prioritize them from most important to least.

Remember, if you're in a relationship, choose your values together as well. You'll never be able to create achievable goals without a foundation built on mutual values.

Have fun discovering what you're made of!

You can download and print the following at: **www.MoneySavvyWoman.com/tools-registration**.

HarMoney

Abundance	Belonging	Consciousness
Acceptance	Benevolence	Conservation
Accessibility	Bliss	Consistency
Accomplishment	Boldness	Contentment
Accountability	Bravery	Continuity
Accuracy	Brilliance	Contribution
Achievement	Calmness	Control
Acknowledgement	Camaraderie	Conviction
Activeness	Candor	Coolness
Adaptability	Capability	Cooperation
Adoration	Care	Cordiality
Advancement	Carefulness	Correctness
Adventure	Celebrity	Country
Affection	Certainty	Courage
Affluence	Challenge	Courtesy
Aggressiveness	Change	Creativity
Agility	Charity	Credibility
Alertness	Charm	Curiosity
Altruism	Chastity	Daring
Amazement	Cheerfulness	Decisiveness
Ambition	Clarity	Decorum
Amusement	Cleanliness	Dependability
Anticipation	Clear-mindedness	Determination
Appreciation	Cleverness	Devotion
Approachability	Closeness	Devoutness
Approval	Comfort	Dignity
Artistry	Commitment	Diligence
Assertiveness	Community	Direction
Assurance	Compassion	Directness
Attentiveness	Competence	Discipline
Attractiveness	Competition	Discovery
Audacity	Completion	Discretion
Availability	Composure	Diversity
Awareness	Concentration	Dominance
Awe	Confidence	Dreaming
Balance	Conformity	Drive
Beauty	Congruency	Duty
Being the best	Connection	Dynamism

HarMoney

Eagerness	Flexibility	Ingenuity
Ease	Flow	Inquisitiveness
Economy	Fluency	Insightfulness
Ecstasy	Focus	Inspiration
Education	Fortitude	Integrity
Effectiveness	Frankness	Intellect
Efficiency	Freedom	Intelligence
Elegance	Friendliness	Intensity
Empathy	Friendship	Intimacy
Encouragement	Frugality	Intrepidness
Endurance	Fun	Introspection
Energy	Generosity	Intuition
Enjoyment	Gentility	Intuitiveness
Entertainment	Giving	Inventiveness
Enthusiasm	Grace	Investing
Environmentalism	Gratitude	Involvement
Ethics	Growth	Joy
Excellence	Guidance	Judiciousness
Excitement	Happiness	Justice
Exhilaration	Harmony	Kindness
Expediency	Health	Knowledge
Experience	Heart	Leadership
Expertise	Helpfulness	Learning
Exploration	Heroism	Liberation
Expressiveness	Holiness	Liberty
Extravagance	Honesty	Liveliness
Exuberance	Honor	Logic
Fairness	Hopefulness	Longevity
Faith	Hospitality	Love
Fame	Humility	Loyalty
Family	Humor	Majesty
Fascination	Hygiene	Making a difference
Fashion	Imagination	Marriage
Fearlessness	Impact	Mastery
Fidelity	Impartiality	Maturity
Fierceness	Independence	Meaning
Financial independence	Individuality	Meekness
Fitness	Influence	Mellowness

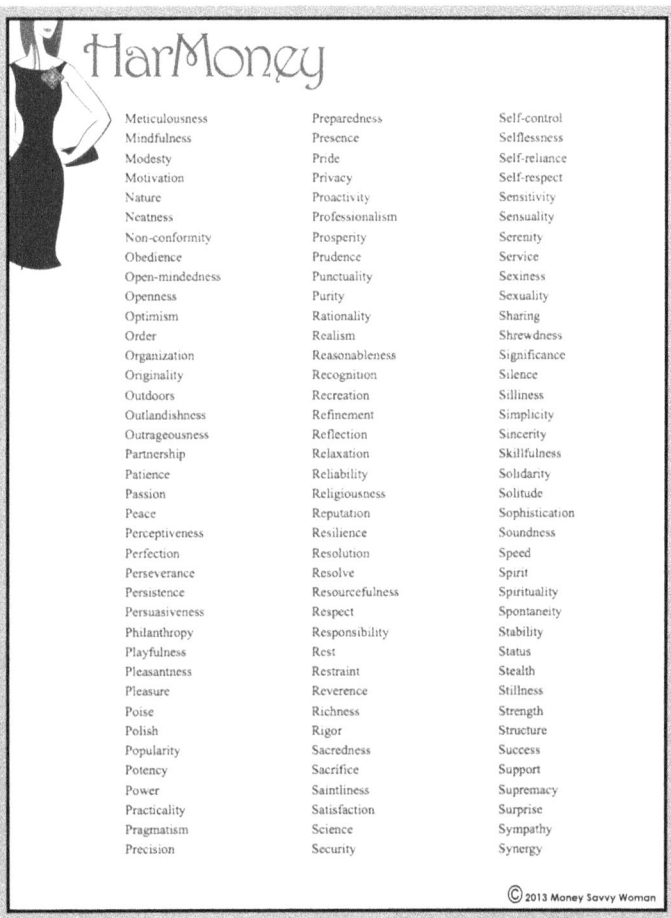

HarMoney

Meticulousness	Preparedness	Self-control
Mindfulness	Presence	Selflessness
Modesty	Pride	Self-reliance
Motivation	Privacy	Self-respect
Nature	Proactivity	Sensitivity
Neatness	Professionalism	Sensuality
Non-conformity	Prosperity	Serenity
Obedience	Prudence	Service
Open-mindedness	Punctuality	Sexiness
Openness	Purity	Sexuality
Optimism	Rationality	Sharing
Order	Realism	Shrewdness
Organization	Reasonableness	Significance
Originality	Recognition	Silence
Outdoors	Recreation	Silliness
Outlandishness	Refinement	Simplicity
Outrageousness	Reflection	Sincerity
Partnership	Relaxation	Skillfulness
Patience	Reliability	Solidarity
Passion	Religiousness	Solitude
Peace	Reputation	Sophistication
Perceptiveness	Resilience	Soundness
Perfection	Resolution	Speed
Perseverance	Resolve	Spirit
Persistence	Resourcefulness	Spirituality
Persuasiveness	Respect	Spontaneity
Philanthropy	Responsibility	Stability
Playfulness	Rest	Status
Pleasantness	Restraint	Stealth
Pleasure	Reverence	Stillness
Poise	Richness	Strength
Polish	Rigor	Structure
Popularity	Sacredness	Success
Potency	Sacrifice	Support
Power	Saintliness	Supremacy
Practicality	Satisfaction	Surprise
Pragmatism	Science	Sympathy
Precision	Security	Synergy

© 2013 Money Savvy Woman

HarMoney

Teaching	Wittiness
Teamwork	Wonder
Temperance	Worthiness
Thankfulness	Youthfulness
Thoroughness	
Thoughtfulness	
Thriftiness	
Tidiness	
Timeliness	
Traditionalism	
Tranquility	
Transcendence	
Trust	
Trustworthiness	
Truth	
Understanding	
Unflappability	
Uniqueness	
Unity	
Usefulness	
Utility	
Valor	
Variety	
Victory	
Vigor	
Virtue	
Vision	
Vitality	
Vivacity	
Volunteering	
Warm-heartedness	
Warmth	
Watchfulness	
Wealth	
Willfulness	
Willingness	
Winning	
Wisdom	

© 2013 Money Savvy Woman

Chapter Three

Creating HarMoneyous Goals

"I don't focus on what I'm up against.
I focus on my goals
and I try to ignore the rest."
~ Venus Williams ~

"And the Lord answered me: 'Write the vision;
make it plain on tablets, so he may run who reads it.
For still the vision awaits its appointed time;
it hastens to the end—it will not lie. If it seems slow,
wait for it; it will surely come; it will not delay.'"
~ Habakkuk 2:2-3 ~

The brooch looked positively stunning on me.

It has to be mine.

My head was spinning. I knew I was going to be out of control.

And then the sales lady teased me, "I just put it out…can't imagine it will be here long."

I knew it was true as I passed by there every day to meet my friends for lunch, and I hadn't seen it.

As if having an out of body experience, I exclaimed, "That's right! It won't be here long because it's going home with me!"

That is NOT What I Wanted

"But I don't *mean* to leave my money in my books, Mom!" I said, drawing out the "mom" as only a 12-year-old could. "It just happens. I work for the Averies on Tuesdays, and on Wednesdays, we go to the library. I always think I'm going to renew my books, but then I forget, and the money's in them!"

Mom had received yet another call from the librarian, and from the scowl on her face, I knew she wasn't too happy with me.

"What about talking to your father? He handles the money for the house; he can help you open a savings account. How about that? Will that work? You should talk to him," she suggested.

"But why are you putting your money in your books in the first place? Don't you carry a wallet or a purse? You carry everything else!" she barked.

Now I feel like a total loser. Not only do I lose my money, but I seemingly don't do what I'm supposed to do! I'm not gonna carry a purse! Really? Only Petra would do that, and she's a 12-year-old woman! I've got better things to do than worry about carrying one of those! The guys would never let me hear the end of it. Where'm I gonna put it? In my softball glove? There's no way I'm gonna be caught dead with a purse! There has to be another way.

"What about talking to your father? He handles the money for the house; he can help you open a savings account. How about that? Will that work? You should talk to him," she suggested. "I know he wants to talk to you about sitting for your brother. You could talk about both matters at the same time and hopefully help each other out."

"I dunno know, Mom. He always seems mad at me," I offered. (Remember, I was 12 going on 13. My dad didn't know what to do with me, as I no longer looked like his little girl, but was transforming into a young woman. He was clearly baffled by the physical changes.)

"Well, this will make him happy. He'll feel you're asking for his help," Mom insisted.

"Okay. If you think it will help, I'll give it a shot," I grabbed a cookie from the cookie jar and headed for my room.

So, I delayed and delayed, carrying around my babysitting money in a blue and white striped gym sock for a few weeks, until I finally got the nerve up to talk to my dad.

There he was, hidden behind his paper, reclined in his chair, after dinner. Everyone was gone except us. I let out a squeak, "Dad…uh, Dad. Mom said you wanted to talk to me about sitting for Dave?"

The paper came down. "Oh, yeah. Let's see. Your mom and I want to bowl with the league on Friday nights. We thought we'd take your sisters if you'd watch your brother. We'd pay you, of course. What do you get paid these days?"

"$2 an hour," I answered.

"Wow. Are you worth it? Seems like $1.50 an hour is more appropriate," he said coldly.

More appropriate? What does that mean? I get $2.00 an hour to watch the Averies' sleeping 3-year-old. What's the difference? I don't get it. Dave is 3.

And as if he read my mind, he continued, "You can stay home, eat your own ice cream, play your own games, watch your own T.V. You don't even have to leave the house. What do you say? $1.50 an hour, for four hours on Friday nights?"

With those sharp words from my father, I gave up my 50 cents an hour, 25% of my monetary value, and a chunk of my self-worth.

Does he think he's doing me a favor? I want to get away from here. Now he's keeping me at home AND cutting my pay? Am I not good enough for him to give me $2 an hour? Everyone else seems to think I am worth it. He never seems to think I'm good enough. But if I don't say "yes," he'll just be angry, and then what?

I really didn't know what to do. Trapped between wanting to please both my mom and my dad, I caved. With those sharp words from my father, I gave up my 50 cents an hour, 25% of my monetary value, and a chunk of my self-worth. "Sure, Dad. It's your Crowned Prince I'm watching," I murmured and slunk away, realizing I'd essentially taken a pay cut to stay home and work.

"Well, he better be for that price!" my father called out from behind his paper.

Then I remembered my need and turned back, "There's something else. Do you think you could help me with a savings account or something? I don't have anywhere to put my money. It keeps disappearing, and Mom says I need to become more responsible. She said you could help me open a bank account for my money."

"Well, I could open an account for you one day after work and put the money you earn from me in there and any you give me. How would that work for you?"

"That sounds great, Dad! Thanks!"

Immediately, I felt like I'd graduated. But all was not as it seemed.

What were some of the messages you received about money and your self-worth, as a child and an adult?

Christmas was approaching, and I was getting excited about buying gifts for my family and friends. With a little spring in my step, I ventured into the garage to ask my dad for some of my money. For nearly two years, I had babysat for several families. I spent some cash on school clothes and other stuff, but regularly had given my dad most of the money. He had also kept what I'd earned from him and put it in my account.

"Dad, I'd like to get some of my money out. Can I go with you to the bank?" I asked.

He ignored me. Not once, not twice, but several times.

I bent down to look under the car, "Dad! I need my money! I want to go to the mall and get my gifts. Let's go to the bank and get my money."

I couldn't believe I had been deceived by my own father.

"I don't have time now, Renée. I'm working on the car." He didn't even look at me.

"Give me the book thing, I'll ride my bike, and get the money myself!"

"You're not old enough! Now let me concentrate on this car!"

"Mom can take me! Tell me where the book is!"

"Damn it, Renée!" and he rolled out from under the car. "There is no passbook! There is no bank account in your name! Now leave me the hell alone! I've got to fix this car or we won't go to church tomorrow!" And with that declaration, I was stunned into silence and disappeared.

I couldn't believe I had been deceived by my own father. The day following our confrontation, he told me he would give me some money, but it never did materialize, and I was too afraid to ask. I was disillusioned by what had transpired between us, and I had begun to feel depressed and worthless. Teenaged gloom and doom was setting in for me.

How did you see money ignored or mismanaged in your childhood?

Christmas Day finally arrived, and it had always been a day that I loved to spend with my dad. He was hilarious on this day, acting like a goofball with a referee whistle, hiding gifts, pulling them out of nowhere, and generally having an out-of-character experience, according to my childhood memories. All of our differences would melt away on this day, and I was really looking forward to it. I had managed to buy Christmas gifts with the babysitting money I had earned and didn't give to him. Giving always made me feel good which is why I wanted to buy gifts for my friends and my teachers, in addition to my family.

I spilled out of bed and scampered down the hallway to the living room. My brother and sisters were excitedly unwrapping gifts, and I began searching for mine. I looked under the tree, but there was nothing there with my name on it from Santa, nor was anyone calling out my name. Feeling confused and fighting the feelings of depression that had been circling my head, I determined to find a solution to my puzzle.

That's when it happened. Dad rolled out the powder blue, Schwinn Varsity 10-speed bike I NEVER wanted, NEVER asked for, and NEVER saw coming.

I nearly threw up. The betrayal was complete. In my young mind, the puzzle pieces fell into place.

"What's this?" I asked, as my eyes stung with tears.

"Your bike!" he said, all excited, with a smile as big as Texas crossing his face and a little glimmer lighting up his eyes.

As much as I tried, I couldn't hide my true feelings. "But I don't want a bike," I could barely choke out.

"Of course you do! You've grown out of your old one. It's time you got a new one!"

"So that's it, huh? My Christmas gift of need? They get things for fun, but I get one of need," I pointed to my siblings. "I'm so glad I've got babysitting money so I can buy what I want," I said with despair, utterly defeated.

"Babysitting money?" He laughed. "What babysitting money? That IS your babysitting money!" He pointed to the bike.

I nearly threw up. The betrayal was complete. In my young mind, the puzzle pieces fell into place. Not only was there no bank account, he had taken my money to buy me a bike he needed me to have so I could get to school because my younger sister needed the one I was currently riding.

Essentially, here I was again...I had been burned by whoever stole from my dresser drawer, and now I had been burned by my dad.

What have been your biggest disappointments around money and those you have asked to help you manage it?

When it comes to kids and money, parents have to build a trusting relationship with their children when teaching about money. Yes, in my story, I trusted my dad. Yes, he said he'd put my money in the bank, in an account like my mom said he would.

But in my case, he didn't. He probably did what most busy parents would do — dump it in their own account and run a separate ledger to keep an accounting of what was actually mine.

Since our relationship was strained, we didn't talk about it. When each Friday night came and went, I didn't *ask*, "How much did I earn tonight and did you put it in my account?" Did I ever check? No. Did he ever discuss it with me? Not once. Not only was I not tracking my money, I gave someone I couldn't trust, control over it.

I didn't take responsibility for what I wanted to do with my money. I didn't tell my father my goals. And because I was 12 and didn't see my parents setting goals, I didn't know better. My plan for this particular Christmas was to not only buy gifts for my family, but to buy special gifts for my classmates and teachers as well. I knew my best friends were buying special gifts and I didn't want to be "left out."

It was a huge mistake to avoid stating my goals to my father. If I'd told him I was excited to have saved "this tracked amount" of money so that I could buy amazing Christmas gifts, maybe it would have occurred to him that I was going to ask for it back. In other words, maybe I made it easier for him to assume control of my money. In the end, it was my money that wound up fulfilling his goals and not mine.

This came at a monumental cost to our relationship. He'd tricked me, stolen from me, and then laughed at me as if I was stupid…and I was his daughter. The imprint had been left…*how much could he have loved me to have done this to me?* He made me feel unworthy of the money I'd earned, unworthy of his love. I felt he had branded me with all of that unworthiness by ridiculing me in front of our entire family. I was devastated.

After forty years and a whole lot of forgiveness, I know that my father was a good man. He was a great man. I was his firstborn — much more than he expected, I think. He left this planet way too soon, certainly before we could settle our differences. In his defense, times were exceedingly hard back then for our family. In hindsight, I'm sure he felt he had no other recourse but to use my babysitting money for Christmas presents, and in the spirit of forgiveness, and remembering how happy my little brother and sisters were, then I suppose it was worth it. I just wish he could have said something, anything, to let me know what was happening at the time.

Today, with the knowledge of a CERTIFIED FINANCIAL PLANNER™ Professional, it makes more sense than not to realize that I may have actually underwritten Christmas when my family was really hard-pressed for cash.

Today, with the knowledge of a CERTIFIED FINANCIAL PLANNER™ Professional, it makes more sense than not to realize that I may have actually underwritten Christmas when my family was really hard-pressed for cash, considering he never gave me a penny of the money I'd actually earned. Perhaps that was one of the reasons he resented me; I seemingly could earn money without much effort while he and my mother struggled. I'll never know. But what I do know is that forgiveness heals all wounds.

What would it take for you to forgive that person and/or yourself for putting them in the position to hurt you?

Help for Parents

Parents, these are money lessons you can unwittingly pass on without realizing by "pinching" your kids' piggy banks. Having my time as a stepparent with two young daughters who had their own piggy banks that my husband, Richard, and I would occasionally raid, I realize that parents can sometimes be in a cash-strapped pickle. However, we, the adults, need to remember that we are BORROWING the money from our children whether we tell them or not, and our responsibility is to return those funds as soon as possible. That loan is probably more important to repay than any other. I remember the urgency we felt to get those dollars back in there before the girls ever knew they were gone.

Goals should be set so that funds are earmarked, or set aside, with an end in mind.

Teaching children how to set goals is vitally important. Doing so while they are young will contribute to their ability to achieve financial success.

1. Discuss what goals are important to your child

2. Decide how your child wants to divide his/her funds towards reaching those goals

3. Find a safe place for the money to grow

For instance, if your 7-year-old wants a specific toy, why not arrange a way for them to earn it? (You can match the funds.) If they can count their money and see it add up, they'll get the idea of how setting a goal, earning and saving money, and reaching that goal works.

Famzoo.com® is a great online resource for helping teach your children the value of money. Check it out. You can approach earning, saving, and giving however you choose with Famzoo®.

My First-Marriage Money-Goal Tango

"What are you doing?" I hollered at my first husband, Richard, from the kitchen. "It's time to eat! Come on, the food is getting cold!"

"I'm trying to figure out how we're going to pay for the tickets to get Cathy to Washington DC!" I heard from the far reaches of the office.

"Well, we can figure it out together over *hot* food, okay?" as I started serving dinner.

"I'm coming..."

That was how most of our goal-setting was done in my first marriage. We knew we wanted to do things, and he whittled away and manipulated the numbers until he figured it out. Then he told me, we either spent the money on the goal, or set it aside and moved to our next goal.

He rushed into the kitchen with spreadsheets in hand. "Okay, here's the plan. This year, we don't go to Laughlin with the gang. We keep Christmas lean, which means — no big gifts for us. But, we can go as chaperones with Cathy and here's the good part — tag on another week to the trip and see New York and Boston! To keep things even between the girls," (I had two stepdaughters), "we can give Lizbit what she needs for after-school sports! Waddya think?" He was really excited.

"I'm *totally* excited! DC and Virginia with Cathy and her class, and then you and I, alone, in New York and Boston? I'm in!"

Often I looked at him, dazed and confused, wondering how we were going to pay for everything. But, I trusted him with our money. I gave him my paychecks, and he did the rest. And we did manage it; we did it a lot.

Money wasn't a bad word in our marriage, like it was for the first few years of my second marriage. We knew it was the fuel that gave us joy and momentum to get the things we wanted for our girls and ourselves. Sometimes we disagreed, but seldom, as we both were honest about what was really important to us (values).

We did, however, have one significant financial argument, which was over gifts — his and mine. It came after our trip to New York where we had been window-shopping on Fifth Avenue. We came to Tiffany's, the famous jewelry store and walked in. My first husband *loved* watches, but I already knew these were too rich for our blood. We were just dreaming, and it was fun, so who cared? I saw this incredible titanium watch that I fell in love with: simple, understated, yet so beautiful. It was

> Often I looked at him, dazed and confused, wondering how we were going to pay for everything. But, I trusted him with our money. I gave him my paychecks, and he did the rest.

$800! Without hesitation, it went right back into the case and I said my goodbyes. But I pined for it afterwards.

One year later, he came out with a surprise, a little blue box from Tiffany's. As he walked into my office, I thought, *What's he doing with a blue box from Tiffany's? How'd he find a Tiffany's?*

"I got something for you," he said.

"Really?" I said half excited, half unsure of what was really happening. I opened the box, and there was my lovely, gorgeous watch. I was thrilled. Then I stopped and asked, "Wait. Why now? What's up? How come you didn't tell me? How did we pay for this?" All the questions flooded me at once.

> That's when I found out the cost of his watch and that he'd wiped out our entire gift savings for the year... for family, Christmas, everything!

And that's when he dropped the bomb. He hadn't told me he'd fallen in love with a watch while on our trip, one that cost double mine, and that he'd been tracking the prices on both of them when he discovered my watch was being discontinued. He felt he had to buy mine right then or else it would be gone forever. He also thought it was a good time to let me know that he bought himself the watch he wanted as well so we could both be having "Christmas" in May.

That's when I found out the cost of his watch and that he'd wiped out our entire gift savings for the year…for family, Christmas, everything!

"You spent how much?" I felt my blood begin to boil.

"Just under three grand with shipping and insurance. They gave me a deal!" He sounded so proud of his deal.

"A deal?!?" I screamed. "What are we going to do for birthday gifts next month, and next quarter…oh, yeah… and Christmas! HELLO! Are you CRAZY?!? Do we have any money in the gift budget at all?"

"Well, I thought I'd pull some money from the home and life insurance until we can make it up," he said defensively.

"And just how do you plan to make it up?" I pressed.

"Um."

"Was this a gift? Or am I supposed to hustle some overtime to bring in extra cash?"

"Well, I guess I'll have to talk to the guys and see if I can cover some shifts," he mumbled.

"Damn it, Richard! I can barely look at this thing now and be happy with it. It wiped us out. YOU wiped us out. Why didn't you talk to me first?"

"Well, I wanted to surprise you and make you happy…"

"But didn't it occur to you that wiping out all of our gift savings was something we should have discussed first?" I cut him off. I was on a roll. "$800 is too much for a watch, in my opinion, and $1600 is absurd! I want to strangle you! I don't feel this was a gift for me. I feel it was a manipulation for you, so you could get what you wanted. There. I've said it. That's how I feel. Here's your watch!" And with that, I gave him back my watch so he could add two watches to his collection and stormed out of the house.

That was a pretty terrible argument, considering we seldom argued. It caused me to mistrust him with the gift money. I felt betrayed. And I felt sad that this beautiful watch that I had loved and dreamed about, and for a brief moment, thought was a true gift, was really nothing but a manipulation — he'd essentially stolen my joy around it. Once I had agreed to accept it, which took a long five weeks, I couldn't look at it for a while without feeling a tinge of melancholy.

This whole transaction was essentially a repeat performance of my childhood babysitting bike! I wasn't clear with my dad about what my goals were — I just gave him total control over my money, and he did what he wanted to do with it. Well guess what? Here I was twenty years later replaying the same scenario: trusting someone I loved implicitly with my money, not taking control of it, but allowing my husband to control the money "for me," then doing what he wanted to do with it. Why was I surprised?

What cycles of financial chaos/pain do you see in your life?

However, this time I got angry and voiced my feelings. I felt like a prize idiot. I was determined not to let that happen again. No. No. NO!

We did resolve it quickly by agreeing to approve gift amounts prior to spending. Yes, it does make "surprises" difficult if they're large ticket items, but no surprise should create a financial setback. Ours did, and we agreed that we weren't going there again.

After this nightmare, we made a great team, one that was excellent at setting and achieving financial goals, repeatedly. The key to success in our relationship was communication and trust when talking about money matters. I did my best to stay within the budget when shopping for the household, and he tracked every cent on an Excel spreadsheet.

But it wasn't long after he and I split that I realized that I still had some muscles of my own to build so I wouldn't sabotage my own personal financial goals.

The Calphalon Catastrophe

As I surveyed my new apartment, with its peach-colored walls that gave me that relaxed feeling the moment I opened the door, and its teeny, tiny kitchen, I said, "Wow, I love this place." I was freshly separated from my husband and feeling free and independent.

The place was wall-to-wall with the heirloom furniture granted me by my mother. I also had the piano, and the few pieces that had come to me after my husband and I split. Plus, I managed to get all my tableware, china, and flatware, but not a stitch of cookware.

I need a couple of saucepans, a frying pan, some cookie sheets, a baking dish, a casserole dish, and a stock pot. If I go all out, I might spend $300 or so with tax.

I headed to Mervyn's to see what I could find. *They usually have boxed sets that are reasonably priced. I'll get one of those*, I said to myself as I headed out the door to the mall.

Once I arrived at the mall, I couldn't find a parking space near Mervyn's and wound up near the entrance of Macy's.

No worries, I'll just cut right through and get a little exercise in.

I walked into Macy's and soon found myself following an aroma of food! I had to follow it! Lo' and behold, it took me straight to the household section with every kitchen item you could imagine and this awesome young man demonstrating the worthiness of the new Calphalon surface on their professional cookware!

AWESOME!!!

"I'm looking for cookware!" I nearly shouted.

This guy was good. He had me eating out of his hand, literally. He showed me an omelet in a 7" omelet pan, veggies sautéed in a 10" fry pan, sauce making in a 1 ½ quart pot, pasta in a 12-quart stock pot with a sleeve to make it super simple to get the pasta out, rice finishing with the veggies in a paella pan, and a wok to make stir-fried rice!

Wow! The gourmet chef inside me was so excited, she could hardly believe what was she was seeing, smelling, and tasting! I got to touch this stuff, see it in action, and even eat the food to see how nice everything turned out.

Pretty soon, I wasn't really me anymore. I was a woman on a high, having an outer body experience! I heard myself saying, "I'll take it!"

"You'll take what, my lady?" he asked so sweetly.

"All of it!" I exclaimed! "And throw in four cookie sheets and cooling racks!" I was giddy with excitement. All I could think about was all the food I was going to be able to create.

It took two carts to wheel the stuff to my car, and five months to pay off my $1100 credit card bill. I really don't remember ever hearing a total or paying for the stuff. I only remember getting caught up in the fantasy the salesman had painted for me.

> Pretty soon, I wasn't really me anymore. I was a woman on a high, having an outer body experience! I heard myself saying, "I'll take it!" I had, in so many words, lost my mind.

It wasn't until much later that I realized this Calphalon Catastrophe was the result of me being emotionally vulnerable after the disintegration of my first marriage, and my desperate attempt to feel like I could take care of myself.

I had, in so many words, lost my mind.

If the ridiculous expenditure wasn't sabotage enough, my stubbornness to correct it by returning some of the products sabotaged me even further. I started my new life with a credit card balance, and that wasn't fun. But, I did have a true heart-to-heart with myself.

Renée, what kind of plan can you create to pay off the bill? It wasn't acceptable to simply pay the minimum balance — I had to pay it off quickly.

And what are you going to do to prevent yourself from going crazy again? It was clear the feeling of sadness and loneliness drove me to do things that weren't good for me.

Here's what I decided to do:

- I took a second job with a catering company on the weekends to help me pay off my bills as quickly as possible. Once my bills were paid off, I could save the income towards my goals.

- The second job kept me out of my apartment and mixing with people so I didn't feel so lonely while I adjusted to being single.

- I took up the hobby of rubber-stamp art. My girlfriends were into it, so we did it together. We shared stamps and supplies, and when I was home, I could work on my projects and not feel alone. I kept my purchases within a budget so my hobby didn't break the bank.

- I made my dogs my buddies. This may sound a little weird, but I couldn't take them into restaurants or bars, so I chose not to spend money there. I had the Cadillac of cookware at home, so I didn't really have an excuse to eat out. And my "buddies" kept me company on walks, at home, and during excursions to the open-air market and the like.

So if you're single and you can't have a conversation around money with someone else, you need to be honest with yourself about your vulnerabilities, limitations, and the potholes you find yourself falling into. You can re-route your path and circumvent the potholes if you see them coming and make a plan, which we will talk more about in the next chapter.

When Is It Time to Say NO?

"I would like to stop our wine club memberships. We really only enjoy one shipment out of four, and we have three memberships. *That's a lot of money!* We could take that money and go to the zinfandel festival and buy all the zin we want for a year!"

"Uh huh," Ron grunted.

"Did you hear me?"

"Yeah. I heard you."

"Well? What do you think?" I looked at him questioningly, trying to hold back my excitement. Heck! I wanted to *go* somewhere!

He just looked at me blankly and said, "I like our wine clubs," and then went out the door to start the BBQ.

I had to think for a moment. *Pick your battles wisely, Renée. What you say next could blow it!*

I had to think for a moment. Pick your battles wisely, Renée. What you say next could blow it!

When he returned, I asked him, "Would you please think about it? Then we should consider a party to drink up all this wine we *don't drink* so we can have some room in the fridge. It would be fun and efficient!" I left the room so he could be alone with his thoughts, and I could be alone with mine. I didn't want a fight, but I wanted to get my points across: we were paying for wine we didn't drink, we had too much of it, and we were not having fun! Some things had to change, and it wasn't just in my personal finances.

Tips for Better Money
Conversations with Your Partner

Honestly, this type of conversation happened to me all the time in my second marriage. We remained members of the wine clubs, we hadn't had the party, but, we did try tasting and pairing more of the other wines. However, when I tried to have THIS money conversation, (about spending money on less satisfaction), he wouldn't have it. He would stonewall me into oblivion when he valued the expenditure and felt I didn't.

So, I came to realize, I had a rational money partner the majority of the time until we reached that values-centric point where he felt I didn't value his choice or make valuable choices myself; that's when my partner broke down the communication. When he wouldn't speak to me about money, I knew he was feeling the conflict that we had and avoided talking about it for fear of flaring emotions.

It took me a long time to figure this out.

Not every woman, all of the time, is fortunate enough to have a husband or significant other that is game to discuss money, whether to take the lead or to follow, and that can be frustrating, often bringing money management to a standstill. This is a lose-lose situation, in the short-run and the long-run, that often ends in financial and emotional disaster if allowed to run unchecked and with abandon.

Should you feel yourself identifying with that scenario, all is not lost. There is hope, and so much of it lies in YOU. You may need to hire a Money Coach or CFP® to make it safe enough for you to have this conversation, but if you think you can get somewhere with your significant other, then here's what I suggest:

First and foremost, take courage. You're reading this book and that puts you in a position to assert yourself.

Ask your partner to do the exercises with you, even if you've already done them. Get them involved. Give them the forms. Praise them for it if they do. Be sincere.

If you can't get a conversation started to begin the process together, then start it yourself and ask for their input either in writing or verbally. Try some phrases like this:

- *"I have some ideas for spending and would like your thoughts. When's a good time to talk?"*

- *"We wanted to go on vacation this year and I have some ideas. Can we spend a little time after dinner Tuesday to discuss it? I'd really like your input."*

- *"You've always got such great ideas on things, how about twenty minutes Thursday evening so we can figure out how to take care of the property tax bill? I'd love your help on this."*

- *"We've got a bit of a situation with our cash flow. Can we take ten minutes to sort it out?"*

In all these examples, you are simply trying to get them involved PAINLESSLY. Smile when you ask. Remember not to have any alcohol to inflate or exaggerate emotions. Keep to the topic at hand. Stick to the time limit. When you're done, you're done.

If talking doesn't work, sometimes putting your ideas in writing and allowing them to make notations draws them in. This allows them to be alone without anyone "judging" them. They are free to say what they really want. I have one client who does all her difficult conversations with her spouse through letters. They communicate much better that way rather than face-to-face; it's too difficult for her husband to say how he really feels in the spoken word; he prefers the written word. They're less defensive, kinder to each other, really think about what the other has taken the time to write, and know that the letters are written out of love — not anger or any other negative emotion.

In either case, start slow. Be kind and gentle. This is a team effort. My conversation with Richard over the watch was a FIGHT. It wasn't constructive until he apologized for blowing the budget without asking and I apologized for the mean things I said that I didn't write in this book.

When communication breaks down, yes, you may get frustrated, because being stonewalled is frustrating. Work towards incremental steps and with time, you should be taking strides towards success, together.

If you find you cannot get through at all, ever, you have a few options. You can choose to handle everything yourself, as long as the element of sabotage doesn't exist. If you cannot handle the affairs alone and need help, or you have been asked to handle the affairs yet your spouse or significant other sabotages your efforts, or you are dependent upon them and they will not communicate with you, then you may just have to deal with the harsh reality that there is a communication block between you that may require some professional help. Go seek it out if the relationship is worth saving before both you and your finances are devastated.

No More "Yes" Girl

"Wow. I feel like I'm running around with my hair on fire," I said, sinking into my chair. I wasn't one for liquid lunches, but this was about as close to one as I was going to get. I sat across from my girlfriend, another businesswoman, and let the cat out of the bag. "Cherie, I'm doing everything my mentors are telling me to do. These folks are pillars of their industries…insurance, investments, retirement, and alternative investments. I'm doing it all! I'm working 70-100 hours a week, my husband never sees me, and I have nothing to show for it." Huge sigh! "I don't even know what's working and what isn't!"

"Well, if you could cut one thing out, what would it be?" she asked.

"All the running around!" I broke down in tears. "I've been all over the country hanging on every word these experts have said and told me to do. I'm tired. I miss my husband, my friends, and my dogs. I want a life, and I don't have a clue where my finances are, AND I'M A FINANCIAL PLANNER!" I wailed.

She let me sit there for a bit not saying a word. Then very calmly she said, "Listen to your own voice, Renée. Stop saying 'yes' to them and say 'yes' to what's important to you. You're the only one that matters in your world. You're spending all of your profit chasing their 'yeses.'"

It hit me like a left hook. I knew exactly what I wanted to do. I just didn't have the confidence to do it until that very moment. For some reason, I felt I lacked something. But in that moment I became angry — angry at myself for not having the confidence to step out on my own, and angry at them for making me feel like I couldn't do it without them. I paid some of them a lot of money for coaching and mentoring. Others didn't charge me, but I paid an arm and a leg in travel to spend time with them. I put myself up for the conference that was "essential" to my success. It was a sobering moment that I'll never forget.

All this time, I'd kept my mentors' goals in sight and not my own. Once that realization hit me, I could follow my own process of being grateful for all the knowledge I'd acquired, achieving the crystal clear clarity of what my values were through my conversation with Cherie and, lastly, develop my own goals for my professional career and not the ones created by my mentor.

I no longer had the "student/teacher" mentality, where I behaved as if their approval was paramount and jumped through any and all hoops they set up for me. I was taking the bull by the horns, creating the business I wanted, using my rules, and doing it my way.

"I've been all over the country hanging on every word these experts have said and told me to do. I'm tired. I miss my husband, my friends, and my dogs. I want a life, and I don't have a clue where my finances are at, AND I'M A FINANCIAL PLANNER!" I wailed.

Remember, your professional life is not your personal life, but you need to apply the same attentiveness to both when it comes to your goals and money matters.

What would it look like for you to "take the bull by the horns" in your personal and professional life?

Resetting Your Mindset:
The Goals Conversation

In this chapter, you've learned that aligning your values with your goals is essential if you ever hope to achieve them, and that it will take some determination and commitment on your part to make it happen. But it doesn't have to be all doom, gloom, and drudgery. It can actually be quite the opposite experience if you approach it as such.

One of the things I see a lot of women struggle with as they create goals is a feeling of unworthiness.

> *Do you have desires or wishes for items or experiences (your goals) but wonder if you are worthy of them? Do you secretly wonder if you can make the goals happen, and whether you and your desires are worth the effort?*

It happens a lot. People spend decades living without reaching their goals, and eventually stop believing that it's possible. And, if they have spent a lot of time punishing themselves for poor financial decisions in the past, then they *really* struggle with the worthiness issue. They don't think they deserve it, and they cut themselves off from the desire because it's too painful to wish for it and never achieve it.

Remember, *you* are worthy of your desires, goals, and dreams. You are worthy of living an extraordinary life, full of fun and abundance.

> People spend decades living without reaching their goals, and eventually stop believing that it's possible.

I Am Worthy of Abundance and Wealth

After anchoring all of your gratitude for what you *do* have and forgiving yourself of your past financial mistakes, you can begin to create goals from a place of worthiness and excitement.

From this feeling of gratitude, abundance, and worthiness, picture your goals in your mind and the feelings they conjure up inside you. Visualize how these goals make you *feel* — the joy, excitement, pride, relaxation…whatever it is, *feel it!* I still feel the joy of my brooch, and when Richard and I were saving for our DC trip with Cathy, it was exhilarating (I had pictures of DC, Boston, & NY everywhere)!

> For example: *See* yourself hugging your family members and friends while on that

dream vacation. *See* your boss vigorously shaking your hand while you accept a huge bonus check and *feel* the pride of knowing you're valued. *See* yourself donating a check to your favorite non-profit. *See* yourself living that perfect day and *feeling that exhale of relief that it's YOUR day and no one else's.*

Tools for HarMoney™: *Set Some Goals*

You can download and print the following at:
www.MoneySavvyWoman.com/tools-registration.

1. **Write your goals down in any order. Think in terms of Needs, Wants, and Wishes.**

   Needs: a "Need" is a goal that has an urgent deadline, or is something we can't live without. (But that doesn't mean because we have goals that are "Needs" we can't work towards goals that are "wants" and "wishes." If that were the case, no one would ever go on vacation or stretch beyond their needs.) Good examples of "Needs" are: new tires because the current ones are bald, your own place, and union dues.

Wants: a "Want" is something that can wait, but you'd really like to have it sooner than later. Say for instance, a new computer, or a new car in *three* years as opposed to *ten* when you will need a new car, or a new home. "Wants" can be very motivating.

Wishes: a "Wish" is something you hope to have someday, but your heart won't break if it takes a while to get or you don't get it at all. Good examples are: joining a posh health club, buying a high-end car, and taking the entire family on a cruise and footing the bill for everyone. As your advisor, I'm going to say that you will be successful in reaching ALL of your goals if you plan, are determined, and committed. But even if some of your wishes are a miss, or near miss, things have a way of working out in the "Wish" department. If one wish fizzles, it's generally because another took its place, usually a better, brighter one!

2. **Using the "EZ GOAL SETTER" form, transfer your goals into the following categories:** Needs first, then Wants, followed by Wishes.

3. **Write the dollar amount necessary to fulfill each goal in the space provided.** Do not guess. Do the research to find the amount to fulfill your goal. If you

want a house or a car, find out how much money you'll actually need for the down payment if that's all you'll need. Use real numbers, not estimations.

4. **Now continue to ponder these goals a while and decide when each of them is going to happen.** Pick a date and then write it in the due date column of the EZ Goal Setter form. This date can be one of necessity, as may be required for a goal of need, or one of fancy, if it is a wish. Once the dates are determined, you then know how long you have to make good on your goal, on your commitment to yourself.

5. **The next step is to prioritize your goals.** This is a two-step process. Prioritize each category: Needs, Wants, & Wishes. Then prioritize the entire list as if the categories didn't exist.

When prioritizing, it's important to know where to start — that's the whole point. But with money, it's important to wrestle the demons of conflict. "What I need" or "What is right" vs. "What I want" is a battle that wages within every normal person.

Compare the two lists. Do you see any differences? If so, what are they? Do you find yourself wanting to forsake much-needed financial goals for the more fun and entertaining goals? Do you find yourself tied to savings and foregoing the fun stuff? This is telltale information about YOU that will help you reveal your stumbling blocks and pitfalls — the things you need to watch out for and keep your eyes on.

6. **Put your goals in order of goal achievement date using Worksheet #2.**

   • Short-Term: up to one year

   • Intermediate: over a year through five years

   • Long-Term: six years or more

   This will give you the perspective of knowing how much cash you're going to need in the short-term, the next 2-6 years, and the long-term. Beware of needing $15,000 in the next year, and then $45,000 in the next five after that. It might be a lofty goal to achieve. This isn't intended to be a dream-killer. If we set goals that are too far out of reach, we might just sabotage ourselves, and give up on any of our goals. We need a head's up on what's coming down the pike and to have a sense of what to do to attain those goals.

7. **Next, determine where you are going to start.** Choose one or two goals to work on directly and start hammering away! But let's set you up to WIN!

   Most people start out with the intention to achieve their goals, but few actually do because they are ill-prepared mentally. They just simply aren't committed. They haven't done the homework to find out if what they want to achieve is actually doable in the amount of time they want to do it by and within the means they currently have available to them. When this harsh reality hits them *unawares*, they quit. The goal is forsaken and they fail. Are you willing to make the necessary commitment(s) to see this through?

8. **Determine what steps you're going to take over the time allotted to meet your goal.** When I bought my brooch, I knew that I had $10 to eat with for two weeks. Yeah, two weeks! I bought three packages of dry-bean soup mix, four pounds of pasta, one pound of butter, a dozen eggs, dented cans of tomatoes, and some celery and carrots. I made the soup for dinner and had the pasta for breakfast with an egg. For lunch I added garlic or some soup to the noodles for variation. I wore my brooch to remind myself why I was doing this. In this case, it was easier as my goal was already achieved. But if you think eating like this was easy, guess again. It wasn't, but I was committed!

When Richard and I were saving for the DC trip, we knew exactly how much overtime he had to pick up, how much side work I had to acquire (I typed screenplays once in a while), and how much of our allotted gift budget we had to put towards travel to make it happen. We were committed. We made the deposit for Cathy and ourselves to go, went to AAA and got the travel guides of NY and Boston to plot out our own trip, put pictures up everywhere to keep our focus, made the additional payments to the tour group as required, and the next thing we knew, we were going!

You can do the same thing. Here are a couple examples:

Buy tires: Shop for the tires you need, price them out including installation, tax, etc. Then figure out how to pay for them using a combination of the following methods:

- *Use savings towards this expenditure (rebuild after you deplete)*

- *Stop most eating out and make meals at home, inexpensively*

- *Look at your Dollars to Sense audit. Where can you immediately cut spending to make this urgent Need goal happen?*

Build an Emergency Fund of $10,000 in 3 years

- *Save $9.15 every day for 3 years*

- *Cut family dinner out ($65) each week for 3 years*

- *Earn an extra $275 a month (ask for a raise, start-up) for 3 years*

9. **Write your game plan down, with all goals and their deadlines.** For instance, with the two goals above, you would probably want to buy the tires as

soon as possible, and work towards that goal first being that safety is of issue, right? Short-term goals can be checked on with each pay-period, as contributions towards them should be made as often as possible.

After that goal is achieved, you would turn to building the emergency fund. That's a more long-term goal and would require that you check that you're on target around the $300 a month saved. If you're nowhere close, you can then go back and see what you need to change to get you the results you want.

At a minimum, have the discipline to check in monthly on your spending and quarterly on your savings. This commitment will pay off in creating good habits of accounting, but also for your accountability in doing what you set out to do. You will be afforded a time to reflect on your values and on your goals—to get that thrill of the big picture and feelings of accomplishment, and then the opportunity to see where you are now, and redirect where you want to go in the future.

10. **Choose the goals you're going to focus on and fit them into your budget.** Review this list every quarter to monitor your progress on your plan.

It's your future, after all, dictated by your goals. If you don't know where you're going ...where are you going?

HarMoney

EZ Goal Setter Worksheet #1

Goal	Need – Want – Wish	Due Date	Dollar Amount	Priority

HarMoney

EZ Goal Setter Worksheet #2

Goal	Due Date	Priority	Dollar Amount

Chapter Four

Establishing Consistent HarMoney

"My sisters and my mom, those people
help me get through every single day."
~ Demi Lovato ~

"Be still, and know that I am God."
~ Psalm 46: 10 ~

I had made the decision that the brooch was going to be mine, and I was willing to do whatever it took to get it.

"How much is it?" I asked, as I looked at my reflection in the mirror, feeling my hands begin to sweat around all of the cash I had for the next two weeks.

"You can wear it out the door for less than $66. A real steal, if you ask me. Look how it makes your eyes shine!" she said, with a warmth that was truly genuine.

The brooch did make my eyes shine. It made my whole face glow. I quickly calculated in my head that I'd only have $10 left to eat with for the next two weeks, but visions flashed before me of how I could do it:

- 2 big scoops of mixed beans for soup cost about $1
- 2 lbs. of pasta for another $1
- 1 dozen eggs on sale $1
- The produce guys would take care of me with the best of what they couldn't sell (they always did when I was cash-strapped)
- I had butter already — I could flavor it with garlic, onion, or cayenne to make the noodles taste better

I could do this. I COULD DO THIS!

"Okay. Yes. Here. $66…and I can wear it out?" I asked, my eyes hardly leaving the mirror.

And I did, in fact, eat eggs, buttered noodles, and bean soup for two weeks while wearing or staring at my brooch.

"Here," Dad said, as he gave me this plastic tube thingy with columns for pennies, nickels, dimes, and quarters. "This is what you can use to save your money in. I want you to put your money here and each Sunday take some out for the Sunday school offering."

We'd been taught to tithe in Sunday school, so 10% was the expectation. But that was it — my big lesson on money. I was 9 or 10-years-old when that happened, and it took all of about a minute standing in the middle of the kitchen.

I never took it seriously because I already had too many quarters from pulling in shopping carts at the local grocery store, and furthermore, there wasn't anywhere to put paper money. I somehow knew already that the system was broken.

Looking back, I realized this plastic holder was a tool to load up coins for rolling and returning them to the bank. Dad and I never got that far in the lesson. I never learned how to make real use of the plastic thingy. Additionally, I never learned how to track how much money I actually had. When my money started to "disappear," I had no clue how much I'd actually lost; therefore, my parents didn't feel they could back me up to put a stop to the stealing of my money.

My system as a child clearly didn't work. My parents, like so many, put little importance on teaching me how to put my earnings on paper, so I would have both the money and a written record of it. They didn't realize that I had no clue how to spend appropriately, save wisely, and give to others to keep the cycle of money moving. My dad didn't realize that there was more to teach me — like how to roll the coins when the dispenser was full, how to give some of it to a cause I cared about, and then how to make a deposit into the bank and watch my account grow.

As a financial professional, it's sad to say, but I never learned to financially crawl, and that makes me sad for everyone else who had the same experience.

As a financial professional, it's sad to say, but I never learned to financially crawl, and that makes me sad for everyone else who had the same experience.

However, looking back, I did seem to figure it out in small, albeit often painful attempts...

The Library System

The Library Bank was my opportunity to learn to financially walk, but it was also a disaster. The librarian was calling my mother, chastising her for my lack of systems, and it was only by the grace of God that my money was returned to me on the occasions that it was.

One would think that my parents would have taken a proactive step in helping me manage my earnings. But that didn't happen. As a result, my money kept slipping through my fingers, instilling messages in me that quickly became hard-wired and difficult to reverse in adulthood.

I had a lot of responsibilities as a child, and using my library book as a cash register when I was 12 seemed like a great idea at the time since it was always with me. I had plenty of singles, fives, tens, and twenties in my book, and the numbers just kept growing until I'd take some out because it was causing a "lump" in my book. I only needed to "make change," after all.

The Purse System

I finally got the message and knew I had to find somewhere else to put my money other than my library books — somewhere where it would be safe, where I could find it when I wanted it, and knew it would be readily available.

"Here," she said, and handed me my first real purse during one of our mother-daughter conversations. It had a wallet for paper money and space for my coin purse. "This will work for now. But you're going to have to speak to your father about this. I can't have you running round with all that cash. How much are you making these days, anyway?" she asked.

"Sometimes $50 a week," I replied, "if you count what Daddy's saving for me."

She didn't seem the least bit fazed. "Now go put your money in your purse and don't make me go into that library again unless it's to go get *my own books!*"

And that was the end of that. By the time she finished her sentence, she was looking at my dress flying out the car door.

I did learn to keep track of my money, by creating my 3-step Purse System:

- Put all money inside purse

- Utilize the pockets for saving and spending, and

- Keep the purse safe — a trick in itself.

I used this system successfully for quite a while. But I knew when I was beginning to work a lot, sometimes as much as four nights a week, several weeks in a row, with an occasional weekend day event that I needed a different system. Mom wanted me to start seriously saving some of it, and I was in a position where I needed to take cash out of my purse because, to quote my mother, "[It] was too much money for a girl my age to be walking around with."

The Dad System

Her attempt to get me some real financial help through my father was genuine and sincere, because we all knew Mom didn't know anything about money. Dad let us all know *that* every time he got paid. And in the bitter end, I wound up with a bicycle and no money at all, which really undermined my financial growth completely. There was no crawling, walking, or running for me. I'd been reduced to rubble. I wasn't worth having money, nor did I deserve it, apparently, according to all of my life experiences up to the age of fifteen.

This is why I want to talk about the family dynamic of money now. When I was a kid, my parents fought about money seven days a week. My dad handled the budget down to an itemized, three-week menu for our family with a correlating shopping list — yes, my father did that because my mother couldn't "be trusted at the supermarket to stay within the budget." And yes, she really was terrible at it. (I handled her money for her in adulthood from the time I was 24 years old until I got married.) I learned that earning money was difficult, that there would never be enough; Dad worked fulltime and my mother worked two jobs. He told us that having children was a burden in some cases, "just another mouth to

I learned that earning money was difficult, that there would never be enough; Dad worked fulltime and my mother worked two jobs.

feed" and that we should wait until we're 28 years old to get married (I waited until I was 29.) He also said you couldn't trust your employer or your industry to keep you employed — guess that's why I started earning my own money, in my own way at such a young age. My mother, on many occasions, reminded me that I could never rely on a man for my financial security, which actually is pretty sage advice, although I think she meant it more as a dig against my father.

The Belief without a System for Action System

The lessons I'd been taught about money were biblically based: "money is the root of all evil," "give 10% of your earnings to the Lord," and "the Lord loves a cheerful giver." But beyond the plastic coin roller, there were no real conversations about money even though I had tried to enter one with my father when I asked for a bank account at my mother's insistence.

Parents need to get on the same page with money, if not for themselves (which is imperative for the marriage to survive), then for their children. My parents used it as a weapon against each other and against me and my siblings. The messages I took away were imbedded in my brain early in indelible ink and stayed there until their painful excavation and eradication decades later in adulthood. For many women, these messages are never removed, let alone detected. For me, they were all related to my lack of worthiness and my inability to manage my own money. This dreadful combination of lies crippled me financially for most of my life. It's amazing what the human brain will do to make a lie the truth if it continues to run rampant unchecked; it will eat you alive—and your finances!

> Couples need to learn how to talk to one another about money and to do so respectfully.

We've all heard the statistic that the number one cause of divorce is related to money. Financial Guru Suze Orman has declared she can predict a couple that's going to divorce by their financials. And I'm sorry to say, she's probably right. Couples need to learn how to talk to one another about money and to do so respectfully. Hopefully, I've given you those tools already and will continue doing so throughout this book.

What systems have you tried before? What worked? What didn't?

The point I want to make is that you need to share this education with your children at the earliest age possible. I started being interested in money at 4 years old. I remember being at my great aunt's house and wanting to earn a dime for helping in the kitchen (I really think my uncle just wanted me out of his T.V. space!). But the lesson needs to be complete with tracking/recording, storage, and delivery. Kids need that help. They also need to celebrate their progress and winning ways, and you are a huge part of that. [**www.Famzoo.com** is an online tool you can use to get your entire family involved in money management. See more in the Resource section at the end of the book!]

The Single Woman System

Yes, this was the time when I had a system and it worked perfectly. It was very, very simple. On a sheet of paper, at the very top, I listed "Income." A few rows down, I listed "Expenses," and on each row beneath that, listed all my expenses starting with rent, then car payment, insurance, electricity, gas, phone, and food. Eventually, I added student loan and credit card. Then I made twenty-six copies of the piece of paper. I used this as a worksheet for each paycheck I got. I had a running record of how much I spent and how much I saved, which was very, very little because I made so little. But I knew I was solvent, and that was a good thing. This is the tool I shared in Chapter 1.

Go to the website now at:
www.MoneySavvyWoman.com/tools-registration.

Every other week, I'd go to the bank, deposit my check, get some cash, and come home and write my bills. It was a ritual – one that was rewarded with a bubble bath afterwards and some solitary "me-time." This worked really well for me until I fell in love and turned everything over to "the man of the house."

Have you ever managed money well on your own?

The following worksheet is a SAMPLE to illustrate how I used it to record my earnings and my expenses. It is a periodic worksheet, so not all of my expenses for the entire month were listed on each one — only the expenses that were meant to be paid with that paycheck.

Note how all of the income since the last paycheck is included. In this scenario, I included a payment from a multilevel business. (For me, it was Mary Kay. For you, it could be vitamins, pre-paid legal, a beauty product, whatever, but record it here along with your other income.) Include yard sales, rebates, and anything you sell through ebay, etc.

Total your earnings. As your bills come in for this period, notate them on the worksheet so you don't miss any and you're aware of what you need to stay ahead of them.

When your paycheck comes in, total the expenses to that date, and subtract your total expenses from your income total. With a positive number, you're free to pay your bills without any concerns.

If you have money left over, you need to decide what to do with it. If the amount is substantial, consider putting it towards your goals. If it's negligible, as in the sample, I throw it in my "Fun Money" account – a stash of cash I keep for mindless spending like the ice cream man, pizza delivery, or a Sunday matinee.

If you're caught short, you'll need to dip into your savings or decide which bills are most important and pay those, pushing the balance to the next pay-period's worksheet.

If you choose NOT to pay a credit card account, YOU MUST CALL THEM AND TELL THEM SO. However, I caution you to pay them something, even if it's only $5.00. Calling them before they call you and delivering a smaller payment puts you in a better light and may save your credit report from complete disparagement.

Make several copies of the worksheet if you choose to use it so you always have the next one on hand.

Good luck. I'm proud of you for taking control of your money and your habits. You're doing great!

HarMoney

SAMPLE INCOME/EXPENSE WORKSHEET

Date: _Pay day_

INCOME SOURCES	AMOUNT	TOTAL
Paycheck	668.32	
Multi-Level business	78.56	
Yard sale	111.50	
Rebate	5.00	
		863.38

EXPENSES	AMOUNT	TOTAL
Car Payment	267.12	
Cell phone	57.42	
Electricity	72.08	
Gas	20.34	
Cash-Groceries	120.00	
Cash-Gasoline	130.00	
Roth Acct	45.00	
Efund	50.00	
Vacation fund	100.00	
		861.96
	Difference: Fun $	1.42

HarMoney

INCOME/EXPENSE WORKSHEET

Date: _____

INCOME SOURCES	AMOUNT	TOTAL

EXPENSES	AMOUNT	TOTAL

The Husband System

I'm not sure why I always gave my financial power away when I was in a relationship, but I did. Not a wise choice if you expect to have any kind of financial foundation to call your own. But in all reality, that's what I'd been taught as a child — my dad handled everything in his marriage to my mother — so why wouldn't the husbands in my marriages handle everything in mine? It took me a long time to unravel this pattern, and perhaps this pattern exists in your family's history as well. Just because that's how it was in the past, doesn't mean it has to be that way now or in the future for you. YOU are the one who decides how to handle YOUR money. You can decide to do things differently. Now is the time to make that change. You can take control just as easily as the man in the family. Or better yet, shared control is the ideal.

> I'm not sure why I always gave my financial power away when I was in a relationship, but I did.

Looking back at this era, again, I made just enough to get by and the rest vaporized or never materialized. The powerful money messages I'd learned and ingrained in myself as a child were reaping their negative results over and over again in adulthood, whether I realized it or not.

Have you ever given the financial management over to your man?

The Separate Accounts System

"I think we should keep separate accounts," Ron said, in an attempt to keep control over his funds, while not making an overt money-grab for mine.

This being my second marriage, I didn't argue. "Whatever you like," I responded and disappeared into the bedroom, not wanting to make waves and feeling the relief that he wasn't a control freak when it came to money. *Whew!* I thought to myself. *That was easier than I thought.*

And so we carried on in this fashion for a couple of years. He spent his money on what he valued, and I did the same. Our wake-up call came when we realized that we had no savings and no common goals, as you've already read about in previous chapters.

Two Systems that Will Make Your Financial Life Easier

A System to Pay Bills

For a while, we paid bills traditionally out of each other's individual checkbooks, but that got old fast. We couldn't keep track of what was actually paid and by whom. We needed to set up a system that would work for both of us since we wanted to maintain our independence, so online banking became our system. We set up bill pay, which was free through the bank and made paying bills on time and designating whose account would be used super easy.

As the bills came in, we decided who was going to pay it, we could go to the online bank accounts, choose which account to pay from, pick the date to pay the bill with the appropriate amount, and hit the approve button. No longer was there any confusion about who was paying for what and when. Bills were paid on time, and we could

I'm looking at an alternative to paper altogether and saving a few trees in the process.

handle it immediately when the bills came in — some were even automated like the mortgage, cable, gas, and electric. We never knew it could be so simple. It was awesome! We loved it (and still do)!

For sure, we had to take the time to sort all this out, but the groundwork had been laid through the conversations we had over our values and goals. We decided that an equal percentage of our paychecks had to go to expenses, and it worked out that if he handled the mortgage, taxes, home insurance, and auto insurance, and I handled all the utilities, it was the same percentage of our incomes. He paid for groceries and entertainment, and I saved for vacations and travel. We both did our own retirement savings and paid for our own gifts. The money was able to be channeled into the appropriate places and transferred into the right "savings" accounts so we could meet our goals. Online banking was the system that got us moving in the right direction. We have since graduated to a couple of online tools and use them for our budgeting, goal-setting, and check register reconciliation. I really like how they make things super easy to review money matters together and print things out at tax time. We can also keep up on our budgets via our smart phones, which is really cool.

How do you pay your bills now? Do you have a system that works for you?

A System to Stay Organized

Another system that needs to be set in place is one to organize all of the financial statements. For years I have used the traditional file folder system with a file folder for my bank statements, brokerage statements, utilities (because I tax deduct them), and my paycheck stubs. All you do is go to the local office supply store and get a small supply of file folders and label them with the titles of the records you're maintaining. Some of these will be monthly statements, but some could be quarterly or annual statements. In any case, you need to have a safe place to store them, where you can be sure to find them when you need them, such as tax time or when you are creating a financial plan.

I personally am tired of the "paper trail," and what I mean by that is, the stacks of years of my financial records that at some point I have to dispose of. This leaves me vulnerable to identity theft if I don't find a safe way to dispose of my records. Think about it;

How do you keep track of your financial information?

your statements all have your address and account numbers on them. Any thief could find their way into your trash and claim this information if you don't dispose of it properly.

One way to do it is to shred it with a crisscross cut shredder. The "strip" style just isn't good enough anymore. (Did you see the movie *Argo?* If so, enough said.)

However, I'm looking at an alternative to paper altogether and saving a few trees in the process. There are online "vaults" for financial documents now. There may or may not be a cost involved, depending on which program you choose. The cost can be outweighed by the benefits of the free service, but you can decide. In either case, you won't have to shred your documents out of fear your identity will be stolen or worry about your hard drive crashing or being hacked into. This is important because all of your financial documents: bank statements, retirement statements, pension statements if you work for a school or municipality, can be sent directly to your vault by the custodian where they are neatly filed away. There isn't any opening of envelopes, scanning, losing the statement, filing the statement, and then finding the statement later for tax purposes.

If this remedy sounds too scary for you, you can always resort to the traditional method of paper files in your file drawer if you remain organized.

How do you keep track of your financial information? Do you have a system that works for you?

"Hi, Renée, it's Bruce. I'm putting your taxes together and I need some information, *more like all of your info –* your income and expenses from the business. Can you get it to me by Friday? Would like to finish your return and get it back to you. Oh, and don't forget your mileage! Thanks."

And with that voicemail, panic ensued. I hadn't worked on establishing a system for my business yet. I knew I was supposed to be doing monthly Income and Expense Reports, but I'd never gotten around to it.

I have income statements from my broker-dealer and the insurance companies I worked with. I've got the income in the bag. Done! And it's even accurate! But my expenses! Nightmare!

They were all over the place. Thank God for business credit card statements that categorized expenses. I had to go through my checking account, the pile of receipts that I threw into a receipt file, and no, it wasn't separated by month. Some were already too faded to read, and I lost that deduction as I didn't have a clue what the receipt was for.

OMGoodness! The mileage!

I had four different systems that year! One was the little book Bruce, my tax preparer, gave me, which started out that year, but it was too small for my too-big writing. The second was my Palm® Pilot system which proved to be a big hassle time-wise to enter, so I gave that up a few months after I started. The third was all the scraps of paper for the meetings I'd gone to when I didn't want to deal with my Palm® Pilot, and the fourth was the clipboard spreadsheet I made that I actually liked, but was still cumbersome. Consolidating all of this was a righteous pain in the butt!

And with that voicemail, panic ensued. I hadn't worked on establishing a system for my business yet.

A job that should have taken an hour to do, took me two days, all because I didn't have systems in place to support me! I vowed never to put myself in that position again.

The Woman Entrepreneur System

So, I'd like to take a minute to talk to the professional ladies out there. You need to have a system. In my past experiences, the only time I really had a system that worked was the pegboard system during my secretarial service. It was great. But now, using something like that would be laughable.

In my financial business, I felt like an octopus on roller skates. I was so busy doing what my mentors, (and I had a few), told me to do, that I didn't take the time to track my income. I know I'm not alone here, so that's why I shared my story. I said "yes" to everything and everyone. And honestly, I didn't know what was working and what wasn't. That's the problem when you don't track your efforts and your results.

In the beginning, when cash is tight, it makes sense to try and do it yourself. But the first expense you should take on is a bookkeeper. They will not lie to you. They will help you set up successful systems. They will tell you what revenue streams are working and which ones are not. Frankly, for me, having a bookkeeper is truly motivating. I don't want her reporting negative numbers to me, would you? The bonus of hiring her is you're free to do what you do best and you don't have to spend any more time looking at the numbers than looking at the bottom line and determining what needs to be done to improve it.

Simply put all of the monthly income and expense documentation in an envelope and send it off.

> The first expense you should take on is a bookkeeper.

Sure, there will be months that are challenging, and maybe even negative. You'll have choices to make. But you can make them with all of the facts and before you get into financial trouble and fall into the depths of financial worry.

Resetting Your Mind Set: *The Systems Conversation*

Yes, your demons will erupt, and they'll do it at the most inopportune times — most likely when you're trying your very hardest. So have a system in place to ward these monsters off before they derail you. If you know that in the past you haven't been able to control yourself in a certain area, create a system to make sure you do.

For example, I was a clothes junkie during my first marriage. Oh boy. And that carried over into my second marriage too. When the Nordstrom summer sale hit, I felt like Wilma and Betty from the Flintstones, and I'd make a run for the store and buy a whole new wardrobe. (See Wilma and Betty here **http://youtu.be/8rqNZAIQH4U)** Why? Because it was ON SALE! Oh brother! I didn't need these clothes — I just liked having everything new and stylish. I was never very good at thinking about my ROTH IRA!

How did I break my habit? It took two years to find one that worked for me. The first year I looked in my closet and realized I had two closets full of clothes and didn't need new clothes. I really needed to get rid of clothes. So that's what I did during the sale; all three days of the sale I tried clothes on, folded them up, and gave them to charity. I even called a friend over to "help me decide if things should stay or go." She convinced me to stay in my process and not bolt off to the store. I felt better.

I Can Ask for Help —
I Don't Have to Do This Alone

There is no shame in asking for help. We all need it in one area or another. We're human. We do some things well, and we have to work really hard to develop good habits in other areas. Everyone has strengths and areas to work on.

It takes courage to ask for help, but it's absolutely necessary in areas where you haven't practiced good habits before. I had to ask my girlfriend for help controlling my shopping demon, but after a few shopping trips with her helping me stay in my budget zone, I was able to practice these good habits without her help.

The second year, I told myself I couldn't buy any new clothes unless I lost weight because my priority in January had been to lose weight, which I had not done, and now I was facing a true health crisis, Type II diabetes. No clothes. Just exercise! I decided that if I lost the 50 pounds that I needed to lose, then next year I could go to the sale. And I did lose the 50 pounds, and I did go to the sale because I really *needed* new clothes! But, I found myself being much more "choosy" and picking fewer pieces. I wasn't out of control; I was in control. I wasn't shooting my wad of saved money. I was building a new wardrobe with classic pieces. It felt good and again, I was proud of myself. You'll feel that way, too! Mark my words, I promise.

On the flip side, don't be discouraged if you fall or even fail. Think of it as failing forward, as a lesson you can learn from. Take all the good out of it, and if there's any way you can rectify the wrong, do it — take the over purchase back, apologize to yourself for the misstep, and get back on track.

Remember to have patience with yourself. It's taken you a while to get to my book; it's going to take a while to find a system you like, can commit to, and can make a habit of using. Don't beat yourself up if you make a mistake or "fall off the wagon." And certainly, don't quit!

Have compassion for yourself as you would for a child. You'd be firm in your resolve that the behavior is NOT acceptable, nor would it be acceptable in the future. But you'd most likely wrap them up in your arms, hug them to smithereens, remind them that you still love them, that they can start again, and maybe even help them fix what was broken.

It's your money, your rules, your way!

What is the first area in which you need to create a system?

Tools for HarMoney™:
Create Your Money System

I like to think of your money system as a three-legged stool:

- Budgeting
- Bill paying
- Filing/Storage Management

When it comes to discovering a budgeting system for you, ask yourself what kind of person you are.

Are you highly analytical—drilling down to the smallest detail? Have you been brought up with a cash system? When planning a budget, there is more than one way to approach it, and knowing who you are and how you work will help you match yourself with the right budgeting system.

So here are three different approaches to budgeting. See which one appeals to you most.

The most time-honored and widely adopted method is the traditional spreadsheet with columns representing months and lines representing expense categories. The categories can be broken down into subcategories as necessary. For example, popular subcategories are Personal and Business. Most of the software programs on the market today use this setup. Using this model, one will project into the future, using data from the past. That means that you estimate what you'll spend in the next year based on what you spent last year.

Another approach is to only budget with the money you currently have, not worrying about forecasting or the past, and when it flows in thereafter. It is different, and I like it. It simplifies the budgeting process and keeps you engaged with your money. Simply put, you only budget with the income you immediately have and put that money to work. It can be done on a spreadsheet, but differently, or with an envelope system. When given the opportunity to budget from this perspective, it can feel like budgeting "into abundance" because of the way these systems naturally build savings.

There's even a third perspective available, since not everyone thinks in terms of spreadsheets. Some folks think about their money in calendar terms — a week out, a month out, 90 days out, etc. Where a spreadsheet speaks to one person, a calendar might speak to another. When using this method, you would plan your income and expenses by date, using a calendar. This system is used by those who really don't like spreadsheets or analysis, but like that it feels like bill paying in the future.

Each approach addresses a different aspect of analysis, some very robust, others with different focuses. Find which one appeals to you.

So, make sure you go to the website and check out my report to discover the software (and coupons) to get you started right away! www.MoneySavvyWoman.com/tools-registration.

Budgeting is necessary, as you really need to be able to track what it is you're going to need now and in the future, and then match your income to those needs. Having the ability to see how often you were able to meet your monthly targets will give you the valuable feedback you need to keep your plans the same or modify them for success in the future. More on this in the next chapter!

Finding an easy way to pay bills takes the pain out of the process and saves a bundle in late fees, and if you do it directly from the bank, seldom if ever will you overdraw your account, saving you those wretched banks fees. But if you prefer a manual system or other, it's up to you. Again, it's your money, your rules, your way!

And last, but not least, is the all-important filing system. With a manual version, you can still come up with numbers at tax-time in a relatively short amount of time if you do your monthly homework and maintenance. With an online system, they do the filing for you. With a few clicks of the mouse, you can send year-end docs to your accountant, along with the necessary notes from you, and be done with it.

There are so many online tools and software programs available to you, that I've put together a summary of those I've reviewed and suggest. I encourage you to go to the Money Savvy Woman website where you can find my report called, "Closing the Gap ~ Your Money, Your Rules, Your Way" and discover which tools sound best suited to your personality type and needs.

Check it out on the website:
www.MoneySavvyWoman.com/tools-registration.

Chapter Five

Sustaining HarMoney, Your Way

"When you get to a place where you understand that love and belonging, your worthiness, is a birthright and not something you have to earn, anything is possible."
~ Brene Brown ~

"For I know the plans I have for you, declares the
Lord, plans for welfare and not for evil,
to give you a future and a hope."
~ Jeremiah 29: 11 ~

It was so worth it. When I wear that brooch today, I still feel the same way I felt when I saw it that first time — happy.

Was buying that brooch acting in a financially responsible way? Probably not. But I was ready to make the sacrifices it took to reach my goal, even if it meant eating only noodles and beans!

The Malibu Bomb

"Honey, I'm so glad you're home!" she exclaimed, as she threw her arms around me.

"Me, too, Mom." I hugged her back.

"We're going to get you all set up, no problem." She smiled as we finished our hug.

I was 19 years old, and had just moved back from living in Arizona for a couple of years. In one week, I'd found a job, rented a studio apartment, and enrolled in college.

My mother was so proud of me, she took me to our favorite place for dinner to celebrate. As we were leaving, she said, "We need to stop at Diane's for a minute."

So we drove to her best friend's house. She promptly parked and went inside while I waited in the car for a few minutes.

I wanted to cry. I finally choked out, "Thanks, Mom," and I slinked into the car hoping no one would recognize me as I drove home. But my head spun. I loved my mother. I couldn't dishonor her by turning down this gift.

As I sat there daydreaming, I heard her call to me, "Renée! Come here." I got out of the car and walked over to where she was leaning on a car that could only be described as a total jalopy.

She was beaming, smiling from ear-to-ear, looking like a model in a car advertisement.

"Isn't it great? Gary (Diane's boyfriend) is *giving* it to us for $600! I'll pay him and you can pay me $50 a month and it'll be paid in a year!" she exclaimed.

She was so thrilled. I was speechless as I stared at a Chevy Malibu with four tires that weren't all the same size! The paint was oxidized, the upholstery was intact, but ready to fall apart, and it really needed to be driven to the junkyard. With my mouth hanging open, I stuttered the words, "I...I...I don't know what to say!"

I wanted to cry. I finally choked out, "Thanks, Mom," and I slinked into the car hoping no one would recognize me as I drove home. But my head spun. I loved my mother. I couldn't dishonor her by turning down this gift. She'd given Gary the money for it, and it was clear that she intended this bucket of bolts to be a gift for me — a gift she intended me to pay her back for over time.

What am I going to do? Make it work, I guess.

And so I did just that. I sunk my first paycheck into two new tires — used ones, as that was all I could afford. Three days later, I realized "The Bomb" sucked a ridiculous amount of oil, so I bought it by the case. The following month, I put in a starter, the month after, an alternator. It needed brakes, and another two tires. It was a total wreck! One day, the darn thing died in the parking lot at school. I didn't have the money to get it fixed or even towed. I abandoned the Bomb right where it was parked before the sucker was ever paid off. Shameful, yes.

It was a good thing I worked fulltime and went to school fulltime. I didn't have time for anything else! Nor did I have the money. The car left me strapped and broke.

My mother's gift of the car essentially set me up to fail. She was well-intentioned, but her lack of foresight and budgeting skills undermined my chance to succeed with the purchase of this car. If my father were in on this deal, he would have nixed it, but unfortunately, that didn't happen. She never got the car checked out by anyone, and the car didn't last nine months. (Word for when buying a used car...always have your mechanic check it over before actually purchasing it. If the seller won't allow you to do so, then DON'T BUY THE CAR!)

I wound up moving out of my apartment because it was too far from school, moved in with a roommate, and took the bus until I could afford another car. I did everything I could to save for the down payment on a new car. But getting it was difficult, as I hadn't established any credit.

> It never dawned on me that all I had to do was look over my shoulder at what had taken place to prepare for what may come.

Eventually, I financed a Datsun B210 hatchback with the help of my second mom, Sandi Scott. She taught me the in's and out's of buying a car from a dealer so I didn't get taken to the cleaners. It was a great little car. The thing ran like clockwork, but it, too, eventually needed tires, oil, brakes, and the occasional clutch — all standard maintenance.

I could have saved for these expected expenses, but the *unexpected* always took me by surprise. I was never prepared for them. Being a smart girl, I should have been able to figure it out having experienced the Bomb, but my childhood experiences overruled reason.

Silly. Stupid. Absurd. The words to describe that behavior could go on forever. I have only myself to blame as I was the one in charge of my money. But the fact is, I was operating in some kind of vacuum. I didn't know what I didn't know, and no amount of ridiculous misadventures seemed to shake me out of this tailspin.

It never dawned on me that all I had to do was look over my shoulder at what had taken place to prepare for what may come.

**What types of expenses
continue to sneak up on you
over and over again?**

The Wake-up Call: Steadfastness

In all of the stories and scenarios presented in this book, the one thing lacking was the steadfastness to stop the madness and take the time to do the *extremely valuable recording of financial data!* I didn't. I didn't understand its value or purpose for decades. It nearly destroyed me personally and professionally.

As a kid, I didn't have a clue how much I earned, so I couldn't say to my parents, "Mom, Dad, 'X amount of money' is missing out of my dresser drawer, and I know that because Denise and I made 30 cents at her closet production on this day, six bucks at pulling in carts at the grocery store on that day, and three dollars picking up rotten fruit at the Carringtons' on Saturday. You can go ask them if you like." Instead, I had no record of any of it and was shooed away like an errant fly.

As a teenager, if I'd tracked the expenses of the Malibu bomb, I would have known it was costing me more to maintain the car than to keep it. I was so wrapped up in keeping the smile on my mom's face that I just kept dumping money into that money pit! My father was a mechanical engineer; he could have told me to turn around and take it back straightaway if I'd only asked for the help. But I didn't. I was stubborn and wasn't going to ask him for anything — another stupid, costly mistake. So, my financial records should have told me what he wasn't able to. But did I keep them? Nope! In hindsight, what I spent on the Bomb was nearly half of the cost of the Datsun I financed!

It wasn't until I joined Mary Kay when I was 23 years old (a back-door gift my father gave me) that I learned to keep financial records. I thought we were going to dinner, but we weren't. It was a surprise. He drove me to Los

Angeles, pulled up in front of Marie Azer's house, popped the trunk, opened my door, handed me two pink bags, and said, "You could sell ice to an Eskimo. Go learn how."

Every week, we'd go to a sales meeting, and I've been involved in several multilevel sales companies, but none like Mary Kay. The motto there was, "Faith first, family second, career third!" We'd open the meeting with gratitude and celebrations for all of the good that had transpired in the course

I learned very quickly that carpooling to meetings was a great idea, don't give away the farm to sell a mascara, and track everything on the weekly plan sheet.

of the week. Then we moved onto the business lesson. This was the most valuable part of the sales meeting for me. I learned how to determine what was selling, what wasn't, my costs of supplies and my giveaways, the cost of my fuel in relation to my mileage and anything that was spent in the course of the week related to my business. I learned very quickly that carpooling to meetings was a great idea, don't give away the farm to sell a mascara, and track everything on the weekly plan sheet. Through the training courses provided me there, I learned how to track my income and expenses. I finally learned! Thank you, Marie Azer and Mary Kay Ash! You women ROCK!

And you can monitor your funds as well. The tracking tools presented in the Dollars to Sense Audit and the outcomes of your budgeting are crucial here, because without them, you can't monitor what you're actually doing financially. How do you know if you're covering your needs? Sure, you may be paying for your monthly needs without problems, but what about the quarterly and annual bills, like insurance and taxes? Do they sneak up on you and pull the financial rug out from under you? This is where your reporting becomes so valuable. Based on what you find in the reports, the modifications can be simple little tweaks.

Ron and I found that simply eating out one less time per week made a HUGE difference in our bottom line each year. That information would never have been realized if we didn't monitor the expenses. We saw where we were eating out, how much we were spending, and on what days. We could address the pattern and modify our behaviors. We noticed on days I taught at school, we went out a lot. That was an extra expense we didn't value, so Ron agreed to cook that night. BINGO! Problem solved, and it's kind of a fun night for us, even if it's a little hectic. We both know we're saving money and that makes it worth it.

There are budget tools out there to help you with this, so you don't have to start from scratch. But the most important thing is to find a rhythm that works for you.

Ron and I talk about money twice a week. At this stage, many times the conversation isn't even a conversation; it's more of an announcement. But the fact is, we're both in-the-know about what is going on with our finances. We no longer cringe when one of us says, "Sit down, we need to talk." I almost look forward to it with anticipation, as if it's a juicy steak I get to bite into.

Where are your biggest pitfalls financially?

Pitfalls to Avoid

Not using your reports. You may not value using a Balance Sheet and/or the Income and Expense Report, but these are the two reports that will tell you how you're doing financially. How else will you know? Sure, your budget is a guideline, but it won't give you hard numbers to tell you how you're actually performing and what your Net Worth really is. And your Net Worth, a measure of your financial health — specifically your financial assets — is what you're ultimately trying to grow. Remember the silly line, "The one who dies with the most toys wins?" Well that was a little joke about someone with the highest Net Worth. You can put these together using software or without. It's simple. In the "Tools" section, you can find out how.

When I say, "Ignorance is an epic fail," I'm really not exaggerating. I had a woman call me in a tearful panic saying she had two calls to make, one to me and the other to a divorce attorney. The anguish in this woman's voice was sobering; it vaporized any levity I had. She quickly stated that due to economic times, she had been working fulltime and a lot of overtime. When she went into her bank to replace her credit card because it cracked, they took it from her and refused to replace it. Her account had been frozen for being over the limit. She didn't know she even had a balance, believing the balance was paid off every month. As it turns out, her husband had become underemployed, didn't have the heart to tell her, and had rung up a substantial credit card bill trying to keep up the façade of fulltime employment. She was devastated by the news of the vast amount of the debt, shocked that her husband would deceive her, and angrier than a wet cat.

> "Maybe. I don't want a divorce. I just can't trust him anymore," she barely spoke above a whisper.

"Do you love him?" I asked. I could hear her softly weep, as I waited for her reply.

"Yes. But I feel so betrayed. I thought I was going to retire in a couple years. I don't see how that's going to happen now," she choked.

"What if you had a system where everything was out in the open? Where both of you knew exactly how much money you had now, and when it was spent, and there were no more secrets? Do you think that would help? And if you knew where you stood financially at any moment you chose to check? Would that make you feel more secure? You BOTH would be in charge. Both of you together."

"Maybe. I don't want a divorce. I just can't trust him anymore," she barely spoke above a whisper.

I invited the two of them to a meeting.

Two days later, they were in my office and we started the process of weaving the trust back together.

"Tell me what your current system is with money," I started the conversation the way I always do. She just stared at me. He couldn't look at me. "Well, maybe I should ask this: Do you have a system around your money? Who generally handles it?"

The husband, slumped in the chair, looking at his knees, slowly raised his hand without a word.

I turned to the wife. "Do you know what is happening with the household money?"

"No. Not really. Sometimes I'll see a bill, but I don't usually know. He handles everything," she said evenly.

"Well," I calmly replied. "This isn't the best of set-ups. Are you open to my suggestions?"

The wife nodded eagerly and the husband spoke to the ground, "I'm open to anything."

"Great!" I said with renewed enthusiasm. "Do I have some tools for you! You both know how to use a computer, right?" And they both nodded their heads. "And you both have smart phones, right?" Again, they nodded their heads. "Super! We're in business!"

Over the next two hours, I laid out the first major steps of getting back on the same financial page:

- Discussing their values. They agreed right on the spot that they valued trust, transparency, debt-reduction, tracking their monies, and teamwork. I gave them the values homework.

- Discussing their goals. They agreed they needed to learn the budgeting software, schedule money talks, work together, and come up with a more finite list of their goals.

- Recommitting to the future. They needed to forgive the past, and work in the present with a schedule to build that faith and communication in each other, especially when fear and doubt come knocking.

"Can you do these things?" I looked them both in the eyes.

I watched a smile creep across the husband's face, and I knew I'd reached his aching soul. "Yes," he said, as he reached for his wife's hand.

With tears in her eyes, she enthusiastically nodded her head, "Yes."

I wanted to fly over my desk and hug them. I nearly cried with them. They had walked in so broken and disjointed, and now they had hope and were joined together. He was actually looking at me and talking with a voice I could hear and she was hopeful.

This moment was one of the proudest of my entire career. She never made the call to the attorney. I chalk that up for a win on my side!

Today, they're working their plan and paying down their debt. When I talk to her, her voice is clear and strong and she knows exactly what's happening with their money. Her husband doesn't hang his head in shame — that wasn't part of the deal. They're in it together as a team. Sure they have work to do, and they know it. But by monitoring their progress, they can see how they're climbing out of the hole they fell into. Together, they've found ways to get out of it faster. I think if you asked them, they might even say that creating their financial reports and working their system has brought them closer together when statistically they should have fallen apart.

Do you worry that ignorance is not bliss, but an epic fail that will land you in some hot water?

One can actually give too much. Yes, I said giving too much. In my experience as an advisor, most women give too much. This is because *they're not tracking their gifts!* Some are giving well above 20% of their income away! (You can pick your jaw up now.) It's true. They give generously to their spiritual home (church, temple, synagogue) and then continue to give to their favorite charities — sometimes the kids — without any thought of the impact on their own family budget. Sorry, ladies, but I'm calling you on the carpet here. To cut to the chase, ladies, you have to get a backbone and just say, "No." There is no crime in saying, "I have a budget for giving, and I'm sorry, but your charity isn't in it this year. Maybe next year." Smile and walk away. Seriously!

> In my experience as an advisor, most women give too much. Some are giving well above 20% of their income away! (You can pick your jaw up now.)

I had one client give "a couple bucks" a day to the homeless woman at her corner convenience store because she felt sorry for her and guilty for having more than she did. My client was struggling to pay her property taxes and couldn't afford to replace her roof. I made her total what she gave away that year. It came to $520 to the woman alone. She also purchased an appliance for her church kitchen, bought a ticket to church camp for a sixth grader, gave to two other charities regularly, and tithed at her church!

Here are some ways to keep the generous giver in line with a budget if it becomes a problem:

- If you tithe to your spiritual home, make your gift and then STOP THERE! When others ask for donations, simply use the statement above. Before or after tax gifts are your call.

- Budget a monthly amount for your charities, make your donations, and you're DONE! Then use the statement above.

- If you are one who gives money to the homeless, budget for it! Keep track! This is where women lose track of what they're doing, and it can become reckless.

God loves a generous giver. Yes, He does. But he doesn't want her or him out on the street because they gave away the farm!

Are you a giver? Which of the above strategies will help you?

As a result, she was spending over $2,500 a month in dinners out because she missed her family! When I asked her what she really wanted, she said, "I just want to spend time around the dinner table with my family. I want to hear them laugh. I'm afraid I'm missing them grow up!"

Dining out is another money zapper! Ron and I limit eating out to three times a week, preferably two. We like Friday-night date night and Sunday breakfast after church. Sometimes we'll break down and go out when we get lazy, but that has to be a cheap-o meal. Watch eating out. Nothing will suck up your money faster than eating out.

Another client who was a super busy entrepreneur also discovered that dining out was breaking her budget. She valued time with family, but she was too tired to cook or deal with food preparation by the time her workday was over. As a result, she was spending over $2,500 a month in dinners out because she missed her family! When I asked her what she really wanted, she said, "I just want to spend time around the dinner table with my family. I want to hear them laugh. I'm afraid I'm missing them grow up!" I wanted to cry for her, her pain was so tangible in that moment.

"What if we had your groceries delivered and dinners were already prepared? All you had to do was pop them in the oven? Would that work?"

She just blinked at me and whispered, "Is that possible?"

"I think so." Now, the kids start dinner when she calls to say she's on her way home and they all make lunches together between dinner and dessert.

Super quick modify with outstanding results! More money is going towards the goals that matter to her, and most importantly, she's spending time with her husband and children, time she thought she was losing.

How often do you eat out, and how much are you actually spending on that food every month?

Cell phone, Internet, land line, television bills. Nowadays you can bundle these services and save a fortune. You can even drop some of these services if you no longer value the expenses. Remember what you learned in your Dollars to Sense Audit. The modifications you make there can save you a minor fortune.

One of my clients needed to replace his cell phone, so he went to one of those club stores and spoke to the carrier for his wireless service. While there, he was able to do all the following:

- buy his cell phone at a $50 discount,
- learn of a shared plan that lowered his overall costs dramatically,

- learn that his company gave him a 17% discount on his wireless bill (he just had to bring in his paycheck to prove it),

- change his landline phone at home to wireless—saving him another $50 or so (and yes, the 17% discount applies to this), and

- change his broadband to a newer and better device for 1 cent!, and because he was using the newer broadband, it dropped from $70 a month down to $20.

His overall bill went from over $400 a month to less than $250!

When I asked him what his wife thought, he just laughed, "She loved me! I gave her the new broadband device as a gift in a bag with feathers (he meant tissue) and everything! It was a good night!" How much did it cost? One penny? So worth the effort of standing there for an hour to figure it all out and going back with his paycheck to get the discount.

The Unexpecteds. Lastly, stuff happens when you least expect it! A tire blows out, a toe gets broken, or you need to make an emergency trip to bring a parent to stay with you. You just don't know what the future holds. You have to go with the flow and modify your plans to meet your needs. If you're on top of things, you've got no real worries, at least not for long, let's hope.

I'll share a recent personal story where I modified my financial plan. My dearest friend's daughter was getting married. Doesn't sound like such a big deal, but they're Indian, and this was going to be a traditional Hindu wedding with five days of celebrations. I love my girlfriend so very much. I knew from the very first casual get together when Manju introduced me as her "sister," that I wasn't going to attend another event in American garb. My husband and I, with the help of my friend Smita, went to a store in Artesia, CA, where they essentially fitted me with a wardrobe appropriate for this event. One outfit for me was several hundred dollars! I wanted to cry, die…all the things a little girl feels like when she's disappointed that she doesn't get to wear her party dress. It was such a shock to see the prices. I so much envisioned wearing a different outfit to each event — not the same one over and over. And let's not forget Ron needed to wear the proper attire, too.

My husband is such a trooper. He knew how much I loved her, how much she loved me, and how long we'd known each other, and it helped that Manju had actually won him over with her Tandoori chicken! He looked at me with his beautiful blue eyes and said, "You know, we have to pay for this with the bathroom renovation money. You'll be wearing your bathroom to the wedding. That's really the only place we can pull this amount of money from right now."

And with all the love in my heart, I leaned over and kissed him right there in the store for all the world to see.

Resetting Your Mindset:
Keep it Real & Modify as Needed

We're all human, and your plan is as ever-evolving as you are. You may find, in time, that your goals shift. Maybe that diamond ring becomes less important than the vacation you want to treat your family to. Maybe the new car needs to be put further down in the list of priorities because one of your children needs help.

Other times, things can become foggy and unclear. Making sure you keep your focus and that you've got clarity around your goals and the means and ways to achieve them is paramount.

I Am Flexible and Can Rewrite My Rules

When you feel like your plan is lifeless, go back and review your values to re-energize it. It's the very foundation on which you stand.

When you need to refresh them,
review The Values List at
http://www.moneysavvywoman.com/tools-registration.

Your values are what tie everything together, especially if you're in this with others. It takes courage to look inside and dare to share if you're a couple. Be honest, calm, and compassionate so the necessary communication can take place to make things happen and maintain your forward momentum.

Having clarity is an essential piece in breathing new life into a dilapidated mindset. It's amazing how it alone can move mountains.

Tools for HarMoney™: *Monitor and Modify*

Now is as perfect a time as any to ask yourself, "What comes up for me emotionally as I take on the role of money manager?"

It's time to make the decision that "ignorance is no longer bliss" and to commit to a schedule of when you're going to address your finances. If you skip this part, you've made the commitment to burying your head in the sand like an ostrich. (Not a pretty picture.)

You are the master of your destiny. You are in total control of your money. Yes, fate does play a role in what goes on, but you are the one who decides how you're going to spend and save your money. By doing the necessary reporting and discovering if you lived according to your plans, only then will you truly be able to reach your goal of financial independence.

So, see yourself completely in control of your money. See yourself during the times you have chosen to do your tracking and monitoring having complete and total success. See yourself easily preparing your reports and determining your next steps towards success.

You can use one of the tracking and monitoring options I shared in Chapter 4, or you can download an easy-to-use Balance Sheet/Income & Expense Report Form from: **www.MoneySavvyWoman.com/tools-registration.**

It's yours for the taking. Believe you can and you will!

Practicing the HarMoneyous Mindset

"You may have to fight a battle
more than once to win it."
~ Margaret Thatcher ~

"I can do all things though
Christ which strengthens me."
~ Philippians 4: 13 ~

The Seminar Seduction

There I sat, mesmerized by her poise, professionalism, polished performance. She was everything I wanted to be. My own coaches have told me, "You need to get in her sandbox and play with her!" But the echoes of past seminar blunders rang in my head.

You've done this so many times before — lunged at products and books, been seduced into buying stuff you didn't necessarily need. What happened, Renée? Why would this be any different? Why did I fall for those people and their books, DVDs, workshops, and retreats? Why wasn't I enough? What does this woman have now that I need to make this financial leap with her? Is her stuff going to fall by the wayside as they all did?

In my past, I didn't know what I wanted. I wasn't clear on my values or goals. To be completely honest, I was following a pied piper of sorts. The speakers and presenters of the past had seduced me with their promises to "make it better," and since I didn't know what "it" was I was truly aiming for or had a clear path towards, much of what I purchased was useless. I just knew I wanted change and to feel better. I also wanted to put the hard work on *their* shoulders, finding the "easy way out" in their products — so I bought them thinking that paying the price would somewhere save me time and effort. BIG MISTAKE! A lot of that stuff is still in the wrappers it came in.

But things are different for me now. I know where I'm going. I need this woman and, more importantly, her knowledge and guidance. I need to learn from her, have conversations with her, and absorb this stuff. This isn't like those other people. This is different. This is truly a stepping stone, a tool in my toolbox. If I don't do this, my clients will lose out on some of the knowledge I could pass on. She believes as I do, in alignment with my philosophies, and she is so much more confident than I am. I really think I need to do this. I won't let this sit unopened on the shelf — I'm making the commitment to do this, to follow through right now!

I chose to move ahead with making a $1400 purchase with this individual. I learned so much from her. I followed through on my commitment, AND after I made that purchase, she offered the opportunity to bring someone with me for free, so I could split the cost. I listened to the audios and read all of her books. And at the end of attending the 3-day event, that's when it happened...

"So now it's time to step up and play with the big boys!" I heard her say, and she launched into the sell of her $13,000 program! "We'll take you through our 12-step process!" *(Yeah, I need a 12-step process all right!)* "We'll give you a process for your business, including an employee manual! We'll get you investing properly! We'll get your marketing plan in place! We'll get your..." My eyes glazed over.

I really wanted to go because she'd helped me so far, I'd learned a lot that transferred very well into my business, and I liked her.

I need to do this to play big! She'll take my little business and make it grow like I can never seem to do. She'll fix it. She'll make it over for me!

I need to do this to play big! She'll take my little business and make it grow like I can never seem to do. She'll fix it. She'll make it over for me!

As the messages raced through my mind, I could feel myself wanting to move to the back of the room. I wanted to make it happen, wanted to join some of the friends I'd made, wanted to be in the VIP room with the rest that had made such a commitment, and I nearly signed up for it.

But something didn't feel right.

I had to think and get my head clear of all the hoopla, and when I did, clarity did come.

Here's what I found:

First of all, I wasn't ready for that huge of an expense financially. It would have been a complete disaster.

But more importantly, when it came down to the level of expertise she was offering then, after a lot of true meditation on it, and prayer, she wasn't the right fit.

Again, I had to battle my inner voices of wanting the easy way out while balancing it with finding the right mentor.

Where have you spent the money for 'an easy way out' and paid a bigger price?

She had proven to be the perfect mentor for mid-level education. But I needed a different mentor to experience the C-level training and guidance which I eventually found in someone who had been with me all along — someone who truly understood me, my business, my strengths, and weaknesses, personally and professionally. If I would have taken the leap without thinking, I would have missed the much deeper relationship of working with the right coach.

Going to conferences and seminars is a good thing. For business owners, they are a fact of life. For individuals, they are motivational and keep us focused on what's important to us. Getting the most out of these events is why we go. But we have to keep our psyches in check.

YOU now have a plan. When you attend these events where they sell at the back of the room, or over the phone or a Lunch and Learn, don't lose your focus.

Ask yourself these questions PRIOR to your participation:

What is my purpose for attending?

Am I here to see anyone in particular? If so, am I here to hear them speak or seek them out as a potential coach or mentor? If the latter, am I prepared to move ahead financially today?

What is my budget for books and DVDs of the people I become acquainted with today? Can I get them cheaper on Amazon? Am I here today solely as a listener? (Know that going in makes it so much more enjoyable to just meet people and ignore the back of the room entirely if it's not in your budget.)

What steps am I going to take to make this conference profitable with, or without, spending money on resources?

Now, you know your purpose; now, convert that to action.

Ready, you can stand firm on your own values and goals, and once you have the answers to the questions above, stay on your own financial path and plan maintaining your integrity, budget, and confidence. Being able to discern *their plan of having you buy their products and services* and your plan of simply gaining vital information is the key to moving from glazed purchaser to champion.

And if you're there to gain the expertise of one of the

presenters, wait for the "deal" they're offering. If they don't offer one, ASK for one since you're prepared to move ahead today!

No more questioning yourself, getting scared, or losing your way. You've already taken care of that by preparing yourself.

Now, go enjoy yourself and have the experience of your life!

CAUTION!!!

Protecting Your Plan

I obviously didn't do a very good job of protecting myself or my plans for most of my life. I was a turtle without a shell, but you don't have to be, nor should you be. My point here is to caution you, warn you, and to say, "BEWARE!" This part is all about protection.

If there's one thing I've learned over the years, it's how quickly a plan can come under attack from anyone, anywhere, once we let people know we have one and how your psyche can need support. Resetting your mindset will be necessary. It may be a big reset, or a little one, but in any case, these tools will be here for you in this book so you can turn right to them when you need them. But let's start with protecting your plan since you've put so much time into putting it together.

Now, I pray that you are surrounded by people who lovingly support you and your goal of becoming financially free and wealthy, but I know that most people reading this book will find themselves surrounded by naysayers, party poopers, even cruel rascals, at home or in the often-misinformed media.

Television Shows – Let me just say, you can learn a lot from television, no doubt. Remember, when it comes to TV, these folks have a job — to fill the hour. Shows like *Squawk Box* (my personal favorite), **The Suze Orman Show,** *MONEY with Melissa Francis, Fast Money*, and *Mad Money,* and the shows on the **Bloomberg** and **FOX** are networks are just a drop in the bucket and great examples of shows that are produced to provide information to the general public. I affectionately call the folks who anchor them, "the talking heads." I tune into some of these rather faithfully because they have a good reputation for presenting data and information from reputable resources, and they're in line with my politics. However, even they have slow news days; I can discern what is fact and what is filler — not necessarily fiction, just non-essential material that doesn't have any bearing on the real issue originally presented.

The question is, do you? I've gotten more than one phone call on a crazy news day when reporters had conflicting reports. In every instance, my question back to my clients was, "Does this have any effect on your plan? Is this something that falls outside of the financial plan we put together?" In almost every case, the answer was, "No." They had just gotten caught up in the scare tactics, fear-mongering, or sensationalism going on in the press.

You should also know when shows give you tips to buy certain securities, generally speaking, your actual ability to "get in" on a winning tip is already gone. This can really infuriate me. I often wonder if the players making recommendations on these shows are making money at your expense. Frankly, they buy the security at a lower price before you even know it exists, and they tell you and the entire world about it. Then, everyone, including you, buys it driving the price up so they can sell it and make a nice, tidy profit. Any chance to make real earnings on it is history once the name is mentioned on the show. However, you *can* learn a lot about how stocks, options, and the management of companies work while watching these shows. Just do your homework on these securities to make sure they're something you truly want to get involved with.

Radio Shows – Radio tends to lean to the sensational, if not out-right insanity. Being that you can only listen to these shows, they tend to really go for shock value to keep you engaged and tuning in on a regular basis. You can learn a lot, but the same story holds true for radio as for television. Your chance to make your full profit is passed by the time they announce the opportunity on the air.

FREE Dinner & Lunch Opportunities – I have a love/hate relationship with these things. When I first went out on my own, I offered this type of opportunity, so I know exactly how it works. There are ethical people out there using this type of advertising to gain clients. However, as an advisor working with my clients, I've come to discover that they were taken to the cleaners when offered trusts and investment opportunities. On more than one occasion, I would attend the meeting set up by my client with the "financial planner" offering an "alternative" or "low cost solution."

See, that's the deal. You get a free meal in return for meeting with the presenter — there's no obligation, but they're pretty persuasive, if not downright manipulative. I've sat in on enough of these to realize my clients were afraid enough to ask me to attend to make sure they didn't get talked into something they didn't want to do — because they already did!

The worst case of all I attended, I literally had to reveal that I wasn't the daughter I was posing to be, but that I was actually a CERTIFIED FINANCIAL PLANNER™ Professional who was there at the request of my client, and they — the salesperson — hadn't honored my client's request to leave as my client didn't need any of the annuities or the reverse mortgage the salesperson came to sell. The products were outrageous! He was being pressured to roll-over his current annuities into different annuities that were 12-17 years in duration, and my client was in his late sixties and ill! The salesperson's presentation was very slick and intimidating. Three times my client told him he already had enough annuities and didn't want anymore. But the salesperson didn't stop and kept going as if my client didn't say a word.

I finally interrupted him, remarking, "I don't think you're listening. He isn't interested in a reverse mortgage. He's said he's not interested in annuities either!"

I then asked if he had anything else to offer. He started in on a reverse mortgage presentation.

"I'm not interested," my client said. "It's time for you to leave."

It took over thirty minutes and a threat to report him to get the salesperson to leave. My client was visibly shaken. I shudder to think what would have happened if I wouldn't have been there. My client was ill-prepared to get rid of him once this unscrupulous salesperson was inside his home as he was frail and soft spoken. I was grateful I was there to save him from himself. God only knows what could have happened if I weren't there to get that creep out of his house. And he went through all this for a free lunch! Really? Think about what you're doing when you get involved with these types of opportunities. If you want to take advantage of an offer, check out the company fully before accepting the invitation and RSVP'ing.

Why do people go to these things when they already have a plan and open themselves up to trouble? Their friends may have asked them to go with them, and maybe they were bored and wanted a free meal. I don't know all of the answers, but those are some my clients have told me.

Trust Mills – The other horror stories are the trust mills. I can't tell you how many of my prospective clients believed they had a living trust after attending one of these presentations for the "low price of $400" or whatever low price they got talked into. When I asked to review it, they delivered a batch of cellophane-wrapped forms that were never even opened, reviewed, or even discussed with them. They were actually under the impression that buying such a packet was all it took. I wound up having the dismal job of informing them that they had been rooked.

Another situation I've frequently come across with trust

mills is where the client did speak to someone over the phone who asked a lot of questions, which they answered, and then sent them a trust packet in the mail. However, the trust was never funded, meaning the assets were never actually transferred from their individual ownership into the trust thereby never gaining the protection the trust was originally intended for.

A living trust needs to be prepared by an attorney, who actually TALKS to you, gets to know you and what you're all about, and will then complete the process by making sure the trust is adequately funded. It's your entire estate and all your assets that you're trying to protect—don't bargain hunt! You need the proper protection, with all of the proper powers, and an attorney who will keep your trust updated with the necessary legislative changes when they happen. It should fit you like a glove!

What your family member/best friend/neighbor just did — I hear about this one the most. Share it with me for sure if it really interests you. But remember, that's *their* plan, not *yours!* Enough said.

What you can say to them is this: "That sounds really interesting. Thank you so much for sharing it with me. I'll be sure to run that by my advisor to make sure it makes sense for me/us. Can you tell me the name of that again?" And write it down. This last part, the writing it down, is the key to shutting the conversation down. If you don't, they will spend the next ten hours trying to convince you that their tip is the best!

The opportunity over the phone that you must take advantage of *NOW!* — These callers are notoriously discovered to be scammers. These callers target seniors and the elderly. Hang up. End of story. There's nothing to say. Again, HANG UP!

Remember, your plan is YOUR plan! Your time, effort, values, and goals are what make it up. It's okay to get an idea and then do some research to find out if a new option may fit into your plan at a later date. But don't shuck your plan for someone else's ideas. You've worked too hard to cast it all aside on someone else's whim.

Your mind is the most valuable asset you've got when you keep it strong. Money is simple, but it can be hard. There are times when it can get the best of you if you're not on top of it. Tools like forgiveness, gratitude, and visualization are all so important to improving your financial health.

Here are the mindset skills and tips to reinforce your intentions, reinvigorate you, and get you back on track and keep you at the top of your game.

I Am Grateful

Make a list of everything you have to be thankful for right now. Start the habit of closing each day with a simple list of five (5) things you're grateful for that day. Gratitude has a way of creating abundance. You'll be amazed at how living in gratitude opens doors to so much good coming your way.

I Am Forgiving

Forgive yourself your mistakes. If you have a setback, it isn't the end of the world, and don't throw the baby out with the bathwater! Stop beating yourself up. You need to forgive yourself and move on.

Remember the saying, "Don't look back. You're not going in that direction anymore!" You have the power to catch yourself and turn yourself around.

Repeat the following line and fill in the blank as many times as you need until you cannot think of another thing to forgive yourself for.

I forgive myself for _____.

Clearing your mind of all anger, regrets, and fears, again, forgiving others and yourself, so you can move on, frees you of all negative self-talk, thinking, and "programming,"

I Am Worthy of Abundance and Wealth

Picture your goals in your mind and the feelings they conjure up inside you. Visualize how these goals make you feel — the joy, excitement, pride, relaxation.

Whatever it is, FEEL it! Capture this feeling and embed it in your brain. Consider making a vision board, a poster with pictures of all your goals on it. Feel yourself having all that you desire.

Remember to have patience with yourself. If you struggle with letting go of the failure, revisit the forgiveness exercise until you're free of your pain and guilt.

Tracking your money is an on-going practice and can be challenging for many. Taking the first few exciting weeks of this newfound knowledge and turning it into habit isn't always as easy as it sounds. I encourage you to take a few minutes to visualize the following at the beginning of your money sessions:

CLOSE YOUR EYES and SEE yourself as the Master of Your Destiny. SEE yourself in TOTAL CONTROL of your money. SEE yourself EASILY preparing your reports and DETERMINING YOUR NEXT STEPS towards success. SEE yourself during the times you have chosen, TRACKING AND MONITORING and having COMPLETE AND TOTAL SUCCESS. SEE yourself PROTECTING yourself and your plan, WARDING OFF SABOTEURS, SKILLFULLY AVOIDING POTHOLES AND PITFALLS, AND CONFIDENTLY DEFENDING YOUR DECISIONS. SEE yourself ALREADY THERE!

Believe you can and you will. Believe in you!

I do!

I Can Ask for Help — I Don't Have to Do This Alone

Yes, your demons will erupt, and they'll do it at the most inopportune times — most likely when you're trying your very hardest. So having a system in place to ward these monsters off before they completely derail you is vital.

If you know that in the past you haven't been able to control yourself in a certain area, create a system to make sure you do now. Remember how I found a friend to distract me during the sales at Nordies? Or when I chose to take advantage of the sales, and kept her there as a guardian of my boundaries that I'd set? You can do the same, and I encourage you to set these healthy boundaries and enlist true family and friends to cheer you on and support you.

On the flip side, don't be discouraged if you fall or even fail. Think of it as failing forward, as a lesson you can learn from. Take all the good out of it, and if there's any way you can rectify the wrong, do it — take the over purchase back, apologize to the one you're in a relationship with, if necessary, and get back on track, and most importantly, forgive yourself. No wallowing, pity parties — okay, maybe a 15-minute pity-party, and be done with it! Take the bull by the horns (that's you!) and make a list of all you're grateful for.

I Am Flexible and Can Rewrite My Rules

We're all human, and your plan is ever-evolving as you are. With time, things can become foggy and unclear. Making sure you keep your focus and that you've got clarity around your goals and the means and ways to achieve them is paramount.

When you feel like your plan is lifeless, go back and review your values to re-energize your plan. It's the very foundation on which you stand.

When you need to refresh them,
review The Values List at
http://www.moneysavvywoman.com/tools-registration.

Your values are what tie everything together. And they become doubly powerful when you are in a relationship. It takes courage to look inside and dare to share if you're a couple. Be honest, calm, and compromising so the necessary communication can take place to make things happen and maintain your forward momentum.

Having clarity is an essential piece in breathing new life into a dilapidated mindset. It's amazing how it alone can move mountains.

Now...

You've seen what's necessary...

You've seen the pitfalls...

You've learned the I AM statements you need to reset your HarMoneyous™ Mindset...

And you may be feeling like you still need help...

A Special Invitation
For Individuals
From Renée

Money Savvy Woman, Inc.

**FREE 30-day Membership in the
Money Savvy University**

*What if you could learn to manage your money and have
fun at the same time?*

*What if you could live the life of your dreams beginning
now?*

If you're ready to get started on your own personal
journey towards financial success and independence, you
don't have to wait!

From reading this book, you already know all of my
money stories and that most of them needed to be re-
written. You also know I had some pretty huge obstacles
to overcome, some that felt insurmountable at times. But
I never gave up during those really difficult times, as I

had some incredibly awesome people supporting me. From doctors, healers, and lawyers to friends, family, and my spouse, and then professional coaches, mentors, and experts — this team enabled my recovery, nurturing and guiding me over the course of several years. It was a journey, but I came out the other side triumphant.

You can too! And I've made it a lot simpler and easier for you with a unique virtual training and coaching community — Money Savvy University™ (MSU) — that provides you with the tools and support you need to implement the Money Savvy HarMoney™ process. Here's what you get:

- Weekly video downloads from me, Renée, designed to explain the monthly Savvy HarMoney™ theme,

- Weekly video or mp3 downloads from Supportive Experts supporting the MSU,

- Monthly Mastermind Call with yours truly and Supportive Experts providing a live Q&A in response to the weekly videos,

- Downloadable tools via pdf files in support of the Money Savvy HarMoney™ Process, and

- Access to the Private Money Savvy University Facebook Community.

If you're ready to start your own journey toward financial success by implementing the Money Savvy HarMoney™

process, then the Money Savvy University is a safe place for you to find your footing, ask your questions, and get the guidance you need to learn what you need to know, and side-step costly mistakes.

As you've already learned from reading my book, maintaining a HarMoneyous™ mindset is key to your success. Knowing how isn't always enough. That's why MSU has included awesome and supportive experts who can give you the well-rounded tools to keep you buoyed up, healthy, and positive, while the MSU Private Facebook community provides the support you need, when you need it.

If you would like to experience the support of MSU and join us for FREE for 30 days, just go to **http://www.MoneySavvyWoman.com/Money-Savvy-University** and sign up. In addition to the training and support, you'll also receive my weekly blogs on money and mindset. Don't wait! This type of support will help change your relationship with money and your life.

If you desire more intense training or support, please visit **www.MoneyMakeoverRetreat.com** to learn more about my Money Savvy HarMoney™ Retreats for women and couples.

As a special gift to you, you will also receive a report: *"5 No-Nonsense Steps to Manage Your Money and Become Debt-Free."*

A Special Invitation

For Couples
From Renée

Money Savvy Woman, Inc.

The Money Savvy Marriage Intervention™

*What if you could finally talk about
your money without an argument?*

*What if you could grow
your financial power exponentially?*

What if it could be easy?

Are you ready to do what it takes to find your way to financial success and independence together? Well, it doesn't have to be hard, and you don't have to wait!

You've already read my stories and know I've been married twice and, in both marriages, had to have difficult money conversations. From tracking, establishing individual and shared values, setting goals, working a system, to collaborating on a modification to the financial plan, I've worked through this process countless times with my husband through health crises, economic downturns, and career shifts. Those experiences gave me everything I needed to develop a program to successfully facilitate Money Savvy Marriage Interventions™.

Money is already an emotional, confusing topic for most people, but add in a second set of lacking money stories, values, emotions, and approaches to problem solving, and you can see why Financial Problems is one of the top five reasons marriages end.

It is possible to get on the same page, and I've made it a lot simpler and easier for you. No need for the painful 'trial and error' process or, worse yet, no process. My Money Savvy Marriage Intervention™ (MSMI) provides you with the tools and support you need to implement the Money Savvy HarMoney™ process inside your marriage, increasing your power potential exponentially from the very first session. Here's what you get:

- Monthly one-on-one coaching meetings with me, Renée, designed to explain the Savvy HarMoney™ Process,

- Tools supporting the MSMI to get you both communicating, increasing that power potential right from the start,

- Downloadable tools via pdf files in support of the Money Savvy HarMoney™ Process,

- Membership into the Money Savvy University™ (MSU),
- Access to the Private Money Savvy University Facebook Community, and
- Unlimited access to me, Renée, through email.

If you're ready to jumpstart your own financial power exponentially by learning to communicate about your money, then the Money Savvy Marriage Intervention™ is a safe place for you both to start that journey, ask your questions, and get the guidance you need to learn what you need to know, side-step costly mistakes, and avoid hurtful arguments.

As you've already learned from reading my book, maintaining a HarMoneyous™ mindset is essential to your marriage and a key to your success. Knowing *how* isn't always enough. If you would like to experience the relief of a Money Savvy Marriage Intervention™, then contact me directly through my contact page to set-up your COMPLIMENTARY ASSESSMENT.

Just go to **http://www.MoneySavvyWoman.com/Contact** and enter your information. Everything is kept confidential. Don't wait! This type of support will help change your marriage, your relationships with money, and your lives.

If you desire an intense, weekend training or support, please visit **www.MoneyMakeoverRetreat.com** to learn more about my Money Savvy HarMoney™ Retreats for couples.

As a special gift to you, you will also receive a report: "5 No-Nonsense Steps to Manage Your Money and Become Debt-Free."

About Renée Cabourne

Renée Cabourne, CFP®, founder of Money Savvy Woman, is an Inspirational Speaker, Financial Advisor, Money Coach, and Author who uses her passion and expertise to help her clients, students, and readers transform their financial confusion and struggle into clarity and an exciting relationship with money. She's also a wife, sister, and friend who understands that true wealth comes when one lives their purpose and nurtures the people in their life that make it meaningful, enjoyable, and abundant.

Her educational background in Entrepreneurialism *(Say-Renée Secretarial Service 1983-99, direct sales Mary Kay Cosmetics- 1983-1993),* Finance *(portfolio administrator for Harold Davidson & Assoc 1987-1988, Site Location and Property Lease Negotiator for Peachtree Fashions 1988-1989),* Civil Service *(Clerk thru Asst. to Dept. City Manager, City of Burbank 1990-2001)*, and Education *(adjunct professor, Chaffey College 2006-present)* provided her with a unique skillset, breadth of knowledge, and the experience necessary to nurture her clients, students, and readers. Mentored by some of the pillars of the financial industry, business-leading experts, and powerful transformational coaches, she has created the Money Savvy HarMONEY™ Process, giving people the ability to manage their money effectively and enjoy the freedom, fulfilling relationships, and the ability to get out of the "lack & consumer" mentalities and on to living lives abundantly. In the last 12 months, many of her clients have moved from living paycheck-to-paycheck to having a savings cushion and making monthly investment contributions.

Renée passionately believes that *everyone* has the right to professional advice, whether they have money to invest or not. She is often heard saying, "If you don't have any, you need to learn how!" Her Money Savvy HarMoney™

Process is delivered through one-on-one coaching, retreats, and her Money Savvy University. She is committed to giving those who are motivated to change their current money position the opportunity to do so through sound financial literacy and positive action.

Renée was a nominee for the 2009 NAWBO-IE Trailblazer Award and the 2009 Los Angeles Business Journal "Women Making a Difference" Award, and the Winner of the 2007 NAWBO-IE A.N.I.T.A. Award.

She resides in southern California with her best friend and husband, Ron, and Trevor and Bella, their two Scottish terrier kids. They enjoy travelling, cycling, reading, golf, and pairing wine with gourmet cooking together. She loves spending time serving her Holy Name of Mary church family and Camp Fire Inland So Cal friends. But, her world lights up especially bright when spending time with her first granddaughter, Vivian.